How To Know
Higher Worlds

CLASSICS IN ANTHROPOSOPHY

HOW TO KNOW
HIGHER WORLDS

RUDOLF STEINER

A Modern Path of Initiation

Translated by CHRISTOPHER BAMFORD

⟐ ANTHROPOSOPHIC PRESS

This volume is a translation of *Wie erlangt man Erkenntnisse der höheren Welten?* (Vol. 10 in the Bibliographic Survey, 1961) published by Rudolf Steiner Verlag, Dornach, Switzerland. The previous translation of this text in English was published as *Knowledge of the Higher Worlds and Its Attainment* by Anthroposophic Press, Hudson, N.Y.

The translator gratefully acknowledges the work of both Sabine H. Seiler whose earlier translation provided the basis for the present version and Eva Knausenberger, who helped check the translation.

Published by Anthroposophic Press, Inc.
3390 Route 9, Hudson, N.Y. 12534

Library of Congress Cataloging-in-Publication Data

Steiner, Rudolf, 1861–1925.
    [Wie erlangt man Erkenntnisse der höheren Welten? English]
    How to know higher worlds : a modern path of initiation /
 Rudolf Steiner : translated by Christopher Bamford and Sabine Seiler.
        p. cm — (Classics in anthroposophy)
    Includes bibliographical references and index.
    ISBN 0-88010-372-8
    1. Anthroposophy. I. Bamford, Christopher. II. Seiler, Sabine H.
 III. Title. IV. Series.
 BP595. S894W45813   1994
 299'.935—dc20   93-38966
                                         CIP

Cover painting and design: Barbara Richey

10 9 8 7 6 5 4 3

Printed in the United States of America

CONTENTS

by Arthur G. Zajonc

We live and act within a world whose deeper aspects are hidden from our physical senses. Yet each of us possesses other faculties which, when cultivated, can lift the veil that separates us from spiritual knowledge. In this book, Rudolf Steiner charts a meditative path that leads both to inner peace and to enhanced powers of soul, and finally to the lifting of that veil. The road is long but secure, and is open to everyone. Its fruits of inner serenity, strength, and wisdom benefit not only the seeker but others as well, and certainly the world stands more than ever in need of insights and actions that are born of the spirit. *How to Know Higher Worlds* is, therefore, not only a personal guide to the spirit, but also a path through self-knowledge to compassionate action in the world.

PREFACE TO THE THIRD EDITION

(The first publication in book form)

This book contains the first part of what originally appeared as a series of articles under the title, "How To Know Higher Worlds."[1] The second part will be published separately later.[2] A work of this kind, however, dealing with the human inner development necessary to perceive supersensible worlds should not come before the public in a new form without some introductory remarks.

What is communicated in this book concerning the development of the human soul is meant to fulfill several different needs. First of all, it is intended to help a person who, though feeling drawn to the findings of spiritual science, is compelled to ask where those who claim to have something to say about the deeper riddles of life get their knowledge. Spiritual science certainly has something to say about such riddles. But if we wish to confirm for ourselves the facts on which its claims are based we must ourselves attain supersensible cognition. That is,

1. *Wie er langt man Erkenntnisse der höheren Welten*? (literally, *How can a person attain insights [cognitions] into higher worlds*?), in the journal *Lucifer-Gnosis*, 13-28, Berlin, 1904-5. In German the present work bears the same title as the series of articles.

2. *The Stages of Higher Knowledge*, Anthroposophic Press, 1967.

we must follow the path of knowledge this book tries to describe.

Yet it would be wrong to think that the communications of spiritual science are worthless for a person with neither the inclination nor the opportunity to follow this path. Naturally, to research these facts one must possess the faculty necessary to enter supersensible worlds. But once these worlds have been researched and the findings communicated, even those who have not themselves perceived the facts can form an adequate judgment of them. Much of what spiritual science presents can, in fact, be easily verified simply by the application of healthy judgment in a completely unbiased way.

Only we must not allow our impartiality to be disturbed by any of the numerous preconceptions so common in human life today. For example, we may easily object that some spiritual scientific observations do not agree with certain modern scientific findings. But in truth there is no scientific finding that contradicts spiritual research. It is easy to *think* this or that piece of scientific evidence contradicts what spiritual science tells us about higher worlds, but only if we have not considered the scientific findings impartially and from every point of view. In fact, we shall find that the more open-mindedly we compare spiritual science with the positive accomplishments of science, the more beautiful we recognize the complete agreement between the two to be.

Admittedly, certain aspects of spiritual science will always more or less escape purely intellectual judgment. Even so, we can easily achieve a right relationship to these aspects too, once we realize that not only reason but also healthy feeling can be the judge of truth. If we do not let sympathy or antipathy toward some particular opinion drive our feeling, but instead allow spiritual scientific insight into supersensible worlds to work upon it in a completely unbiased way, then we will find that an appropriate feeling-judgment of the truth results.

Besides healthy feeling of this kind, there are still other ways by which those who cannot, or do not wish to, walk the path to supersensible knowledge can verify spiritual scientific insights. Such people can feel the value of these insights for their lives, even if they experience them only secondhand in the communications of spiritual researchers. While we cannot all instantly become "seers," the cognitive insights of a person who has such vision can nevertheless provide healthy food for all. All of us can apply these insights to our lives; and if we do so, we shall soon realize not only the possibilities of life in every area but also what life lacks when we exclude these insights. Indeed, rightly applied to our lives, insight into the supersensible worlds proves to be far from impractical but rather practical in the highest degree.

Those who do not wish to walk this cognitive path to higher knowledge themselves may well ask, if they are interested in the insights it offers, "How does a seer arrive at these facts?" This book seeks to provide such people with a picture of what must be done if one wishes to know the supersensible worlds. It tries to describe the spiritual path so that even those who do not undertake it themselves can have confidence in what is said by those who do. Once we become aware of what spiritual researchers do, we may find that it makes sense. The description of their path to the higher worlds may impress us in such a way that we understand why the reports of their findings seem enlightening to us. Thus this book may serve those readers who want to strengthen and confirm their sense of truth, and their feeling for the truth, with regard to the supersensible world.

But this book also offers guidance to those seeking a path to supersensible knowledge. Such people will be best able to test the truth of what the book contains by realizing it in themselves. If this is the intention, one should never forget that reading a description of soul development demands more than just knowing the contents of a book—which is often all we strive for when reading other works. Instead, one must live one's way into such a description, and form a close, intimate relationship with it. We should begin by assuming that no single thing will be understood solely on the basis of what is said explicitly about it; rather we will have to come to understand this thing through many other statements concerning quite different topics. In this way we will realize that what is essential does not lie in any single truth, but in the agreement between all.

This process must be taken especially seriously by anyone carrying out the exercises. Although we may understand and practice an exercise correctly, this may yet have the wrong effect unless another exercise is added to it to resolve the one-sidedness of the first into harmony in the soul.

If we read this book closely, so that reading it becomes an inner experience, we will not only come to know its contents, but different passages will also evoke different feelings. These feelings indicate the significance of these different passages for our own soul development and help us to discover how to adapt the various exercises to our own individual natures.

Reading a book like this, in which processes are described that have to be experienced to be understood, a reader will often find it necessary to return repeatedly to the text in order to reread the descriptions. If we do this, we will soon become convinced that we can reach a satisfactory understanding only when we have actually tried something for ourselves—for, having done so, we will notice certain subtleties in the description that escaped our notice on first reading.

Readers who do not intend to follow the path described here will nevertheless find much that is useful for their inner life—precepts for the conduct of life, explanations of what has always seemed mysterious, and so on. Those, on the other hand, who already have certain experiences behind them and have in many respects been initiated by life itself, will find a certain satisfaction in seeing things coherently explained that they had already thought about separately—things they already knew, without perhaps having brought this knowledge into full understanding.

Rudolf Steiner
Berlin, 1909

PREFACE TO THE FIFTH EDITION

How To Know Higher Worlds: A Modern Path of Initiation was written more than ten years ago, and it has been thoroughly reworked in every detail for this new edition. The need for such reworking arises naturally enough in the case of information concerning experiences and paths of the soul such as those given in this book. Every aspect of a work of this kind remains inwardly bound to its author's soul and contains something that continues to work on within it. It could hardly be otherwise, then, that this continuing soul work should be accompanied by a striving to make the descriptions originally presented many years ago clearer and more accessible. Indeed, it was out of this striving that the work on this new edition arose.

All essential elements of the exposition, all the major points have been left as they were. Nevertheless, important changes have been made. I have been able to achieve a more precise characterization of details in many places. This seemed important to me, for if one wants to apply what is communicated in this book to one's own spiritual life it is important that the paths of the soul that are described should be envisaged by the reader as exactly as possible.

Descriptions of inner, spiritual processes are much more liable to misunderstanding than descriptions of events in the physical world. Such misunderstandings arise easily because the life of the soul is in constant movement and because we fail to bear in mind that the life of the soul is very different from life in the physical world. Therefore, in preparing this new edition I have focused on those parts of this book that may give rise to such misunderstandings and have made every effort in my reworking to prevent them.

When I first wrote the articles gathered in this volume, much of the material had to be presented differently, because many of the insights into the spiritual worlds that I have published in the last decade were not yet made public and could only be hinted at. For example, ten years ago I had to refer to the spiritual processes described in my books *Occult Science, The Spiritual Guidance of the Individual and Humanity, A Road to Self-Knowledge*, and particularly *The Threshold of the Spiritual World* differently than seems appropriate now that these works have been made available.[1] At the time of the articles, I could not speak of many things that have since been made public; instead, I had to refer to "oral communication" for more information about these things. Today, much of what was referred to in this way has been published.

---

1. Rudolf Steiner, *An Outline of Occult Science* (Hudson, NY: Anthroposophic Press, 1989); *The Spiritual Guidance of the Individual and Humanity* (Hudson, NY: Anthroposophic Press, 1992); *A Road to Self-Knowledge & The Threshold of the Spiritual World* (London: Rudolf Steiner Press, 1975).

Unfortunately, these comments may have led some readers to a misunderstanding: they may have been led to believe that the personal relationship to a teacher was more essential for those seeking spiritual schooling than it really is. I hope that my emphasis on certain details in this new edition will make quite clear that for people seeking spiritual schooling under the current spiritual conditions a totally *direct* relationship to the objective spiritual world is more important than a relationship with the personality of a teacher. Indeed, in spiritual training, the spiritual teacher today increasingly takes on a merely helping role, just as in accordance with contemporary educational philosophy ordinary teachers in other fields of knowledge are expected to do.

I hope I have sufficiently stressed that neither the authority of the teacher nor the students' trust in the teacher should be any more important in spiritual schooling than in any other area of knowledge or life. It seems to me important that we get a better understanding of this relationship between spiritual researchers and those who develop an interest in their findings. Thus, I trust I have improved this book in all areas where it seemed to me after ten years to need improvement.

This first volume will be followed by a second one that will offer additional discussions of the soul state that enables us to experience the higher worlds.[2]

The new edition of this book was printed and ready

---

2. Such a volume never appeared. The only "continuation" remains *The Stages of Higher Knowledge.*

for sale when the great war, now being experienced by humanity broke out. Writing this preface, my soul is deeply stirred by this fateful event.

Rudolf Steiner
Berlin
September 7, 1914

The new edition of this book seemed to me to require only minor changes. Nevertheless, I have added an afterword to this edition in which I endeavored to explain more clearly than before the psychological foundations necessary to understand it correctly. This afterword also shows opponents of anthroposophical spiritual science that they can hold fast to their view only because they take this spiritual science to be something completely different than what it really is. The true nature of spiritual science, however, they do not even take into consideration.

Rudolf Steiner
May, 1918

*As an aid to readers wishing to follow the text in German,
the numbers that appear at the beginning of paragraphs
indicate Rudolf Steiner's original paragraphing
in the German edition.*

CHAPTER 1

HOW TO KNOW
HIGHER WORLDS

Conditions

1. The capacities by which we can gain insights into
higher worlds lie dormant within each one of us. Mystics,
gnostics, and theosophists have always spoken of a world
of soul and spirit that is as real to them as the world we
can see with our eyes and touch with our hands. Listening
to them, we can say to ourselves at every moment: "I
know that I, too, can experience what they talk about, if
only I unfold certain forces within me that today still lie
dormant there." All we need to know is how to begin to
develop these faculties for ourselves.

Only those who have already developed such powers
for themselves can help us to do this. From the beginning
of the human race, a form of schooling has always existed
in which persons possessing higher faculties guide those
who seek to develop these faculties for themselves. Such
schooling is called *esoteric* or *mystery* schooling; and the

instruction one receives there is called esoteric or occult teaching.

By their very nature, these terms invite misunderstanding. Hearing them, we might easily be led to believe that those who provide this kind of schooling wish to form a privileged class of human beings who arbitrarily withhold their knowledge from their fellows. We might even think that perhaps there is nothing much to this kind of knowledge. Were it genuine knowledge, we are tempted to think, there would be no need to make a secret of it; it could be made public and its benefits shared by all.

2. Those initiated into the nature of esoteric knowledge are not in the least surprised that the uninitiated should think like this. After all, the secret of initiation can be understood only by those who have themselves, to some degree, undergone initiation into the higher mysteries of existence. How, we may well wonder, under these conditions, are the uninitiated to develop any human interest whatsoever in this so-called occult knowledge? Why and how should one seek for something of whose nature one can have no clear idea?

Such questions are based on a completely false idea of the nature of esoteric knowledge. In actuality, esoteric or inner knowledge is no different from other kinds of human knowledge and ability. It is a mystery for the average person only to the extent that writing is a mystery for those who have not yet learned to write. Just as, given the right teaching methods, anyone can learn to write, so too anyone can become a student of esoteric knowledge, and, yes, even a teacher of it, if he or she follows the appropriate path. Ordinary knowledge and ability differ from esoteric knowledge in one respect only. A person may not have the possibility of learning to write because of the cultural conditions or poverty he or she is born into, but no one who seeks sincerely will find any barriers to achieving knowledge and abilities in the higher worlds.

3. Many people believe that they must seek out masters of higher knowledge wherever such masters may be found in order to receive teachings from them. There is a twofold truth to this. On the one hand, if our aspiration to higher knowledge is sincere, we will certainly spare no effort and avoid no obstacle in our quest for an initiate able to lead us into the higher mysteries of the world. On the other hand, we can be certain that, if our striving for knowledge is sincere and worthy, initiation will find us whatever the circumstances. There is a universal law among initiates that the knowledge due a seeker cannot be withheld. But there is also another universal law that esoteric knowledge may not be imparted to anyone not qualified to receive it. The more perfect the initiate, the more strictly these two laws are observed.

The spiritual bond uniting all initiates is not an outward one, but the two laws just mentioned are what hold its members together. You may live in close friendship with one who has been initiated, but until you yourself have been initiated something will always separate you from that initiate's inmost being. You may enjoy an initiate's full heart and love, but the initiate will not share the secret with you until you are ready. You may flatter, you may torment, but nothing will induce the initiate to betray anything that should not be divulged to you if, at the present stage of your development, you do not yet understand how to prepare a proper welcome for this secret in your soul.

4. Quite specific methods prepare us to receive such secrets. Their course is traced out with indelible, eternal letters in the spiritual worlds where initiates preserve the higher secrets. In ancient, prehistoric times, the temples of the spirit were outwardly visible, but today, when our life has become so unspiritual, they no longer exist where we can see them with our physical eyes. Yet spiritually they are still present everywhere, and whoever seeks can find them.

5. Only within our own souls can one find the means of opening an initiate's mouth. But before one can receive the highest treasures of the spirit, one must develop definite inner qualities to a specific high degree.

6. We begin with a fundamental mood of soul. Spiritual researchers call this basic attitude *the path of reverence*, of devotion to truth and knowledge. Only those who have acquired this fundamental mood or attitude can become pupils in an esoteric school. Anyone with any experience in this area knows that those who later become students of esoteric knowledge demonstrate this gift for reverence in childhood. Some children look up to those whom they revere with a holy awe. Their profound respect for these people works into the deepest recesses of their hearts and forbids any thoughts of criticism or opposition to arise. Such children grow up into young people who enjoy looking up to something that fills them

with reverence. Many of these young people become students of esoteric knowledge.

If you have ever stood before the door of someone you revered, filled with holy awe as you turned the doorknob to enter for the first time a room that was a "holy place" for you, then the feeling you experienced at that moment is the seed that can later blossom into your becoming a student in an occult, esoteric school. To be gifted with the potential for such feelings is a blessing for every young person.

We should not fear that such feelings of reverence lead to subservience and slavery; on the contrary, a child's reverence for others develops into a reverence for truth and knowledge. Experience teaches that we know best how to hold our heads high in freedom if we have learned to feel reverence when it is appropriate—and it is appropriate whenever it flows from the depths of the heart.

7. We will not find the inner strength to evolve to a higher level if we do not inwardly develop this profound feeling that there is something higher than ourselves. Initiates found the strength to lift themselves to the heights of knowledge only because they first guided their hearts into the depths of veneration and devotion. Only a person who has passed through the gate of humility can ascend to the heights of the spirit.

To attain true knowledge, you must first learn to respect this knowledge.

We certainly have the right to turn our eyes toward the light, but we must earn this right. Spiritual life has its laws just as physical life does. Rub a glass rod with the appropriate substance and it becomes electrified—that is, the glass rod will now have the power to attract small particles. This process demonstrates a physical law. If one has learned some elementary physics, one knows that this is so. Similarly, if one knows the fundamentals of esoteric science, one knows that every feeling of *true* devotion unfolded in the soul produces an inner strength or force that sooner or later leads to knowledge.

8. Whoever possesses an innate tendency toward feelings of devotion, or has been lucky enough to receive an education that cultivated those feelings, is well prepared in later life to seek the way to higher knowledge. Those who do not bring this preparation with them will have to work at developing this devotional mood with vigorous self-discipline; if not, they will encounter difficulties after taking only the first few steps on the path of knowledge. In our time it is particularly important to focus complete attention on this point. Our civilization is more inclined to criticize, judge, and condemn than to feel devotion and selfless veneration. Our children criticize far more than they respect or revere. But just as surely as every feeling of devotion and reverence nurtures the soul's powers for higher knowledge, so every act of criticism and judgment drives these powers away. This is not meant to imply anything against our civilization—our concern here is not to criticize it. After all, we owe the greatness of our culture precisely to our ability to make critical, self-confident human judgments and to our principle of "testing all and keeping the best." Modern science, industry, transportation, commerce, law—all these would never have developed without the

universal exercise of our critical faculty and standards of judgment. But the price of this gain in outer culture has been a corresponding loss in higher knowledge and spiritual life. Therefore we must never forget that higher knowledge has to do with revering truth and insight and not with revering people.

9. Nevertheless, we must be clear about one thing. Those completely immersed in the superficial civilization of our day will find it particularly difficult to work their way to cognition of the higher worlds. To do so, they will have to work energetically upon themselves. In times when the material conditions of life were still simple, spiritual progress was easier. What was revered and held sacred stood out more clearly from the rest of the world. In an age of criticism, on the other hand, ideals are degraded. Reverence, awe, adoration, and wonder are replaced by other feelings—they are pushed more and more into the background. As a result, everyday life offers very few opportunities for their development. Anyone seeking higher knowledge must create these feelings inwardly, instilling them in the soul. This cannot be done by studying. It can be done only by living.

If we wish to become esoteric students, we must train ourselves vigorously in the mood of devotion. We must seek—in all things around us, in all our experiences—for what can arouse our admiration and respect. If I meet other people and criticize their weaknesses, I rob myself of higher cognitive power. But if I try to enter deeply and lovingly into another person's good qualities, I gather in that force.

Disciples of this occult path must always bear in mind the need to cultivate such admiration and respect. Experienced spiritual researchers know what strength they gain by always looking for the good in everything and withholding their critical judgment. This practice should not remain simply an outer rule of life, but must take hold of the innermost part of the soul. It lies in our hands to perfect ourselves and gradually transform ourselves completely. But this transformation must take place in our innermost depths, in our thinking. Showing respect outwardly in our relations with other beings is not enough; we must carry this respect into our thoughts.

Therefore we must begin our inner schooling by bringing devotion into our thought life. We must guard against disrespectful, disparaging, and criticizing thoughts. We must try to practice reverence and devotion in our thinking at all times.

10. Each moment that we spend becoming aware of whatever derogatory, judgmental, and critical opinions still remain in our consciousness brings us closer to higher knowledge. We advance even more quickly if, in such moments, we fill our consciousness with admiration, respect, and reverence for the world and life. Anyone experienced in these things knows that such moments awaken forces in us that otherwise remain dormant. Filling our consciousness in this way opens our spiritual eyes. We begin to see things around us that we could not see before. We begin to realize that previously we saw only a part of the world surrounding us. We begin to see our fellow human beings in a different way than we did before.

Naturally, this rule of life alone does not yet enable us to perceive what, for example, is called the human aura. For this, still higher schooling is needed. Yet we cannot begin such schooling until we have undergone a vigorous training in devotion.[1]

11. As occult pupils, we should embark upon "the path of knowledge" quietly, unnoticed by the outer world. No one should perceive any change in us. We continue to carry out our duties and attend to our business just as before. Changes occur only in the inner part of the soul, which is withdrawn from, and invisible to, the outer eye. At first, a basic mood of devotion to everything truly worthy of reverence suffuses our entire inner life. This one fundamental feeling becomes the center of our soul's life. Just as the sun's rays quicken all living things, so the reverence in us quickens all the feelings in our soul.

12. At first glance, it is not easy to believe that feelings of reverence and respect are in any way connected with knowledge. This is because we tend to see cognition as an isolated faculty that has no connection whatsoever with anything else going on in our souls. Thus we forget that it is the soul that cognizes. What food is to the body, feelings are to the soul. If we feed the body stones instead of bread, it will cease to function. It is the same with the

---

1. The "Path of Knowledge" is described in a general way in the last section of my *Theosophy: An Introduction to the Spiritual Processes at Work in Human Life and in the Cosmos* (Hudson, NY: Anthroposophic Press, 1994). My intention in the present work is to discuss certain practical aspects in greater detail.

soul. We nourish it with reverence, respect, and devotion. These make the soul healthy and strong, particularly for the activity of knowing. Disrespect, antipathy, and disparaging admirable things, on the other hand, paralyze and slay our cognitive activities.

For spiritual researchers these soul realities are visible in the aura. A soul that learns feelings of devotion and reverence changes its aura. Certain spiritual yellow-red or brown-red colors, as they may be called, disappear and are replaced by tones of blue-red. Our cognitive capacity increases. We now receive information about facts in our environment of which we were previously unaware. Reverence awakens a power of sympathy in the soul. This draws toward us qualities in the beings around us that would otherwise remain hidden.

13. What we attain through devotion becomes even more effective when another kind of feeling is added. This consists in our learning to surrender ourselves less and less to the impressions of the outer world and develop instead an active inner life. If we chase after amusements and rush from one sense impression to the next, we will not find the way to esoteric knowledge. Not that occult students should become dull or unfeeling toward the outer world; rather, *a rich inner life* should orient us in responding to impressions.

A person rich in feeling and deep of soul who passes through a beautiful mountain landscape will have a different experience from one whose inner life is poor in feeling. Inner experience is the only key to the beauties of the outer world. It depends upon the inner lives we have developed whether, when we travel across the ocean, only a few inner experiences pass through our souls, or we sense the eternal language of the world spirit and understand the mysterious riddles of creation. To develop a meaningful relationship to the outer world we must learn to work with our own feelings and ideas. The world around us is filled everywhere with the glory of God, but we have to experience the divine in our own souls before we can find it in our surroundings.

As students of occult knowledge, we are told to create moments in life when we can withdraw into ourselves in silence and solitude. In these moments, we should not give ourselves up to our own concerns. To do so would lead to the opposite of what we are striving for. Instead, in such moments, we should allow what we have experienced—what the outer world has told us—to linger on in utter stillness. In these quiet moments, every flower, every animal, and every action will disclose mysteries undreamed of. This prepares us to receive new sense impressions of the outer world with eyes quite different than before.

If we seek only to enjoy—consume—one sense impression after another, we will blunt our capacity for cognition. If, on the other hand, we allow the experience of pleasure to reveal something to us, we will nurture and educate our cognitive capacities. For this to happen, we must learn to let the pleasure (the impression) linger on within us while we renounce any further enjoyment (new impression) and assimilate and digest with inner activity the past experience that we have enjoyed.

Here we must face a great hurdle, and with it a great danger. Instead of working inwardly we can fall into the opposite and indulge our enjoyment to the full. We should not underestimate the boundless sources of error opening up for us here. For we must pass through a throng of tempters of the soul, all of whom seek to harden the I and enclose it in itself.

As students, it is our task to open the I to the world. And because the outer world can approach us only through sensory impressions, we must certainly seek for pleasure there. If we become indifferent to enjoyment, we become like plants that can no longer draw nourishment from their environment. On the other hand, if we stop at mere pleasure, we become shut up in ourselves. We might have meaning for *ourselves*, but we will have none for the world. No matter how intensely we live in ourselves and how much we cultivate our "I," the world will then cut us out. As far as the world is concerned, we shall be dead.

As esoteric students, we regard pleasure only as a means whereby we can become nobler for the sake of the world. Pleasure becomes a messenger, instructing us about the world. After we have taken in the teaching it provides, we move on to inner work. The purpose is not to accumulate learning as our own private store of knowledge, but to place what we have learned in the service of the world.

14. One fundamental principle of esoteric science, taught in every form of schooling, must never be violated if we wish to achieve our goal: *Every insight that you seek only to enrich your own store of learning and to accumulate treasure for yourself alone leads you from your path,*

but every insight that you seek in order to become more mature on the path of the ennoblement of humanity and world evolution brings you one step forward. This fundamental law must always be observed. Only if we make it the guiding principle of our lives can we call ourselves genuine seekers after higher knowledge.

This truth of esoteric schooling may be summarized as follows: *Every idea that does not become an ideal for you kills a force in your soul, but every idea that becomes an ideal for you creates forces of life within you.*

Inner Peace

15. At the beginning of esoteric training, the student is directed first to the path of *reverence* and to the development of an *inner life.* Spiritual science then provides *practical rules* which, when observed, help us to follow this path and develop an inner life. These practical rules are not arbitrary. They are based on age-old experience and wisdom. They are given in a similar manner wherever ways to higher knowledge are taught. All true teachers of spiritual life agree upon the content of these rules, though they may not always express them in the same words. Any apparent differences are only minor and are due to facts we need not discuss here.

16. No teacher of spiritual life exercises dominion over other human beings by means of such rules. Such teachers do not seek to restrict anyone's autonomy. Indeed, there is no better judge and guardian of human independence than a spiritual researcher. As we said earlier, a spiritual bond

connects all initiates, and two laws hold this bond together. But when initiates leave their closed spiritual circle and appear in public, they are immediately subject to a third law: "Regulate each of your words and actions so that you do not interfere with anyone's free decisions and will."

17. Once we have realized that a true teacher of spiritual life must be thoroughly permeated by this attitude, we know that we can lose nothing of our independence if we follow the practical rules we are given.

18. One of the first rules may now be put into words, somewhat as follows: "Create moments of inner peace for yourself, and in these moments learn to *distinguish the essential from the inessential.*" Here, as I said, it is put into words, but originally all the rules and teachings of spiritual science were given symbolically in a sign language. Whoever would learn the full meaning and import of these rules must first understand this symbolic language. Such understanding, however, depends upon having taken the first steps in spiritual science. To take these steps, one must observe closely the rules presented here. The way stands open to anyone whose will is sincere.

19. The rule concerning moments of inner peace is simple. Following it is also simple. However, the rule leads to results only when the practice of it is as sincere and rigorous as it is simple. Therefore it will be plainly stated how this rule is to be followed.

20. As students of the spirit, we must set aside a brief period of time in daily life in which to focus on things that are quite different from the objects of our daily activity. The kind of activity we engage in must also differ from

what occupies the rest of our day. This is not to say, however, that what we do in the minutes we have set aside is unconnected with the content of our daily work. On the contrary, we soon realize that, if approached in the right way, such moments give us the full strength for completing our daily tasks. We need not fear that following this rule will actually take time away from our duties. If someone really cannot spare any more time, five minutes a day are sufficient. What matters is how those five minutes are used.

21. In these moments we should tear ourselves completely out of our everyday life. Our thinking and feeling lives should have a quite different coloring than they usually have. We should allow our joys, sorrows, worries, experiences, and actions to pass before our soul. But our attitude toward these should be one of looking at everything we have experienced from a higher point of view. Consider, in ordinary life, how differently we perceive what other people have experienced or done from the way we perceive what we ourselves have experienced or done. This must be so. We are still interwoven with what we experience or do, but we are only onlookers of other people's experiences or acts. In the time we have set aside for ourselves, then, we must strive to view and judge our own experiences and actions as though they belonged to another person.

For example, imagine you have had a serious misfortune. You naturally regard your own misfortune differently than you would that of another person. This attitude is quite justified; it is simply human nature. Indeed, it comes into play not only in exceptional circumstances but also in the events of everyday life.

As students of higher knowledge we must find the strength to view ourselves as we would view strangers. We must face ourselves with the inner tranquillity of a judge. If we achieve this, our own experiences will reveal themselves in a new light. As long as we are still woven into our experiences, and stand within them, we will remain as attached to the nonessential as to the essential. But once we have attained the inner peace of the overview, the nonessential separates itself from the essential. Sorrow and joy, every thought, every decision will look different when we stand over against ourselves in this way.

It is as though we spent the whole day somewhere and saw everything, small and large, at close range, and then in the evening climbed a neighboring hill and enjoyed an overview of the whole place at once. Then the various parts of the town and their relationships to each other would appear very different from when we stood among them.

Of course, one cannot succeed in achieving such a transcendent perspective toward whatever experience destiny daily brings us—nor is it necessary to do so. However, as students of the spiritual life, we must strive to develop this attitude toward events that occurred in the past. The value of such inner, peace-filled self-contemplation depends less upon what one contemplates and more upon finding the inner strength that such inner calm develops.

22. For all human beings, in addition to what we may call the ordinary, everyday self, also bear within themselves a higher self or *higher human being*. This higher

human being remains concealed until it is awakened. And it can be awakened only as each of us, individually, awakens it within ourselves. Until then, the higher faculties that are latent within each one of us and that lead to supersensible knowledge remain hidden.

23. We must continue to observe this rule seriously and faithfully until we feel the fruits of inner calm and tranquillity. For each of us who does this, a day will come when all around will become bright with spirit. Then, to eyes we did not know we had, a whole new world will be revealed.

24. Nothing needs to change in our outer lives because we begin to follow this rule. We carry out our duties as before. In the beginning, too, we endure the same sufferings and experience the same joys. We must not in any way become alienated from "life." On the contrary, we become able to live "life" more fully the rest of the day, just because we are acquiring a "higher life" in those moments we set aside.

As this "higher life" makes its influence more and more felt in our ordinary, established lives, the calm of our contemplative moments begins to affect our everyday existence. Our whole being becomes more peaceful. We act with greater confidence and certainty in all our undertakings. We do not lose composure in the face of all kinds of events. Slowly, as we continue on the path, we increasingly come to guide ourselves, as it were, rather than allowing ourselves to be led by circumstances and outer influences. Before long, we realize that the moments set aside each day are a great source of strength for us.

For example, we gradually cease to become angry about the things that used to annoy us, and are no longer afraid of many things that used to frighten us. Instead, we acquire a whole new outlook on life. Hitherto we may have approached what we had to do hesitantly, saying to ourselves, "Oh, I don't have the strength to do this as I would like to." Now, however, such thoughts no longer occur to us. We are more likely to say, "I shall gather up my strength and do my task as well as I possibly can." We suppress any thought that could make us tentative, because we know that hesitation can lead to a poorer performance, or at least can do nothing to improve the execution of what we have to do.

Thus thought after thought, fruitful and beneficial for the affairs of our lives, begins to permeate our interpretation of life. These new thoughts replace the thoughts that previously weakened and hindered us. In the process, we begin to steer a safe and steady course through the ups and downs of life, rather than being tossed about by them.

25. Such inner calm and certainty affect our whole nature. Our inner person grows, and with it, inner faculties that lead to higher knowledge. As we progress in this direction, we become increasingly able to control the effect that impressions from the outer world have upon us. For example, we may hear someone say something to hurt or anger us. Before we began esoteric training, this would have made us feel hurt or anger. Now, however, because we are on the path of inner development, we can take the hurtful or annoying sting out of another's words before it finds its way into our inner being. Another

example: before beginning to follow this path, we may have been quick to lose our patience when we had to wait for something. But now, having started on the path and become pupils in a school of esoteric study, we imbue ourselves in our contemplative moments so fully with the realization that most impatience is futile that, whenever we feel any impatience, it immediately calls this realization to mind. The impatience that was about to take root thus disappears, and the time we would otherwise have wasted in expressions of impatience can now be filled with some useful observation that we may make while we wait.

26. We should realize the scope and significance of all these changes. The "higher self" within us evolves continuously. Only such inner calm and certainty as has been described can ensure that its evolution unfolds organically. If we are not masters of our own lives but are ruled by life, then the waves of outer life press in upon our inner self from all sides, and we are like a plant trying to grow in the cleft of a rock. Unless it is given more space, the plant will be stunted. Outer forces cannot create the space our inner being needs to grow. Only the inner calm we create in the soul can do so. Outer circumstances can change only our outer life situation—they can never awaken the "spiritual person" within. As esoteric students, we ourselves must give birth to a new, higher being within us.

27. This higher self then becomes the inner ruler, directing the affairs of the outer person with a sure hand. As long as the outer being has the upper hand and guides us, the "inner" self remains its slave and cannot unfold

its powers. If other people can make me angry, I am not the master of myself—or rather, better stated, I have not yet found the "inner ruler." In other words, I must develop the inner faculty of allowing the impressions of the outer world to reach me only in ways that I myself have chosen. Only if I do this, can I become a student of the occult.

Only a person striving sincerely for this ability can reach the goal. How far we advance in a certain amount of time is unimportant; what matters is only that our seeking be sincere. Many work on themselves for years without noticeable progress, and then suddenly—if they have not despaired, but have remained unshakable—they attain the "inner victory."

28. Of course, in many life situations, great strength is needed to create such moments of inner peace. But the greater the effort required, the more meaningful the achievement accomplished. On the path to knowledge all depends upon whether we can face ourselves and all our deeds and actions energetically, with inner truthfulness and uncompromising honesty, as though we were strangers to ourselves.

29. Yet the birth of our *own* higher self marks only one side of our inner activity. Something else is also needed. When we look upon ourselves as strangers it is still only *ourselves* that we are contemplating. We see the experiences and actions connected to us by the particular course of life we have grown through. But we must go beyond that. We must rise to see the purely human level that no longer has anything to do with our own particular

situation. We must reach the point of contemplating those things that concern us as human beings as such, completely independent of the circumstances and conditions of our particular life.

As we do this, something comes to life in us that transcends what is personal or individual. Our view is directed toward worlds higher than those our everyday life brings us. We begin to feel, to experience, that we belong to these higher worlds of which our senses and everyday activities can tell us nothing. The center of our being shifts inward. We listen to the voices that speak within us in our moments of serenity. Inwardly, we associate with the spiritual world. Removed from our daily round, we become deaf to its noise. Everything around us grows still. We put aside everything that reminds us of outer impressions. Quiet, inward contemplation and dialog with the purely spiritual world completely fill our soul.

For students of the spirit, this quiet contemplation must become a necessity of life. At first, we are wholly absorbed in a world of thought. We must develop a *living feeling* for this silent thinking activity. We must learn to love what streams toward us from the spirit. Then we shall soon cease to accept this world of thought as less real than the everyday life surrounding us. Instead, we will begin to work with our thoughts as we do with material objects. And then the moment will approach when we begin to realize that what is revealed to us in the silence of inner thinking activity is more real than the physical objects around us. We experience that *life* speaks in this world of thoughts.

We realize that thoughts are not mere shadow pictures and that hidden *beings* speak to us through thoughts. Out of the silence something begins to speak to us. Previously we could hear speech only with our ears, but now words resound in our souls. An inner speech, an inner word, is disclosed to us. The first time we experience this we feel supremely blessed. Our outer world is suffused with an inner light. A second life begins for us. A divine, bliss-bestowing world streams through us.

30. This life of the soul in thoughts, gradually broadening into life in spiritual beingness, is called in spiritual science or gnosis "meditation" (contemplative reflection). Meditation, in this sense, is the way to supersensible knowledge.

We should not lose ourselves in feelings in these moments of meditation. Nor should our souls be filled with vague sensations. This would only keep us from attaining true spiritual insight. Our thoughts should be clear, sharp, precise. We will find a way of achieving this if we do not stay blindly with the thoughts arising within us. Rather, we should fill ourselves with high thoughts that more advanced and spiritually inspired souls have thought in similar moments. Here our starting point should be writings that have themselves grown out of meditative revelations. We may find such texts in works of mystical, gnostic, or spiritual scientific literature. These texts provide the material for our meditations. After all, it is seekers of the spirit who have themselves set down the thoughts of divine science in such works. Indeed, it is through these messengers that the spirit has permitted these thoughts to be made known to the world.

31. Practicing such meditation will completely transform us. We begin to form quite new ideas about reality. Things take on a different value for us. Yet such transformation does not make us unworldly. In no way does it estrange us from our daily responsibilities. This path teaches us that the most trivial tasks we have to carry out and the most trivial experiences that come our way are woven together with great cosmic beings and world events. Once this interconnection becomes clear to us in our moments of contemplation, we will enter our daily round of activities with new and increased strength, because now we know that all our work and all our suffering are work and suffering for the sake of a great, spiritual, cosmic interrelationship. Thus meditation produces not indifference but *strength* for life.

32. Consequently, students of higher knowledge walk through life with confidence, holding their heads high, regardless of what life may bring them. Before, they did not know why they worked and suffered. Now they know.

Naturally, such meditative activity will lead to its goal more easily if it is practiced under the guidance of someone with experience who knows from personal knowledge how best to do it. Therefore, we would do well to consider the advice and instructions of such people. We certainly will not thereby lose our freedom or independence. Such guidance turns uncertain groping into work with a clear end. If we listen to those with knowledge and experience we will never ask for guidance in vain. Nevertheless, we must understand that we are seeking only the advice of a friend, not domination by someone who wants to have power over us. We will always find that those who truly know are the most humble and that nothing is more alien to them than any lust for power.

33. When we raise ourselves through meditation to what unites us with the spirit, we quicken something within us that is eternal and unlimited by birth and death. Once we have experienced this eternal part in us, we can no longer doubt its existence. Meditation is thus the way to knowing and beholding the eternal, indestructible, essential center of our being. Only meditation can lead us to this vision. Gnosis and spiritual science speak of the immortality of this essence and of its reincarnation. It is often asked why we do not know anything of our experiences before birth and after death. This is the wrong question. Rather, we should ask how we can attain such knowledge.

Meditation, properly carried out, opens the way to such knowledge. Meditation brings to life memories of experiences that lie beyond birth and death. Each of us can attain this knowledge; each of us possesses the capacities to see firsthand what true mysticism, spiritual science, anthroposophy, and gnosis teach. We have but to choose the right means. Only a being with ears and eyes can perceive sounds and colors. But even the eye can see nothing when the light that makes things visible is lacking. Spiritual science offers us a method of developing our spiritual ears and eyes and of kindling the spiritual light.

Three stages in this method of spiritual schooling may be distinguished: (1) *Preparation*, which develops our spiritual senses; (2) *Illumination*, which kindles the spiritual light; and (3) *Initiation*, which initiates our relationship with higher spiritual beings. These stages will be discussed in the following chapters.

CHAPTER 2

THE STAGES
OF INITIATION

1. The following information forms part of a spiritual training, whose name and essential nature will become clear to anyone who makes use of it in the right way. It concerns the three stages by which the school of spiritual life leads to a certain degree of initiation. But only those explanations that may be made public will be found here. They are indications derived from a much deeper, more intimate teaching.

In the esoteric school, from which these communications are drawn, the student follows a definite course of instruction. Specific tasks and exercises are used there to bring the human soul into a conscious relationship with the spiritual world. These more esoteric practices compare with those presented here as instruction given in a rigorously disciplined higher school or college compares with what is taught incidentally as preparation in a lower school. Yet the *sincere* and unwavering pursuit of what is intimated here nevertheless leads to real esoteric training.

Impatient experimentation, without sincerity and persistence, however, will get us nowhere. We can succeed in esoteric study only when the indications given in the previous chapter are observed and made the foundation of further work.

2. Three stages of initiation are described in the tradition from which this schooling derives: preparation; illumination; and initiation. These three stages do not follow each other so rigidly that it is absolutely necessary to complete one stage fully before going on to the next. A person may receive illumination, and even initiation, in relation to some things, while remaining at the stage of preparation in relation to others. Nevertheless, a student must spend a certain amount of time in preparation before the stage of illumination can begin, and only after illumination has taken place—at least regarding certain things—can initiation begin. For simplicity's sake, however, the description that follows will discuss the three stages in sequence.

Preparation

3. The stage of preparation consists in a quite definite method of cultivating our lives of feeling and thinking. Just as natural forces equip the physical body with organs fashioned from unstructured living matter, so the care and cultivation of our lives of feeling and thinking endow our soul and spiritual bodies with higher senses and organs of activity.

4. The first step is to direct the soul's attention toward certain processes in the world around us. These processes

are life, as it buds, grows, and flourishes; and, on the other hand, all phenomena connected with withering, fading, and dying away. Wherever we turn our eyes, these two processes are present together. By their nature, they always evoke feelings and thoughts in us. Normally, however, we do not give ourselves sufficiently to these feelings and thoughts. We rush from one sense impression to the next. Now, however, we must consciously and intensively focus our full attention on them. Whenever we perceive a quite definite form of blossoming and flourishing, we must banish all else from our souls and, for a short time, dwell on this one impression alone.

As we do so, we will soon realize that a feeling that previously only flitted through our souls has now grown and become strong and filled with energy. We must let this feeling quietly echo within us. We must become inwardly completely still. Cutting ourselves off from the rest of the world around us, we must attend only to what the soul has to tell us about the facts of blossoming and flourishing.

5. But attending to our souls in this way should not lead us to believe that we shall advance far on the path if we blunt our senses to the world. First, we must look at things as actively and precisely as possible. Only thereafter should we devote ourselves to the feelings coming to life in our souls and the thoughts arising there. It is essential that we give our attention to both feelings and thoughts as they arise in complete inner equilibrium.

If we find the necessary inner peace, surrendering ourselves to what comes to life in our souls, then after a certain time we will experience the following. We will notice rising up within us new kinds of feelings and thoughts that we never knew before. The more often we focus our attention, first on something growing and flourishing, and then on something withering and dying away, the more lively and active these feelings will become. Eventually, just as the eyes and ears of our physical organism are formed by natural forces out of inanimate matter, so organs of clairvoyant "seeing" are formed out of the feelings and thoughts that arise in relation to growing and flourishing, withering and dying.

If we cultivate our feeling life in this way, we will find that a specific form of feeling is attached to processes of growing and becoming, while quite another is attached to those of withering and dying. These forms of feeling may be described, but only approximately. Each student may obtain a complete idea of them, however, by going through the inner experience. Whoever repeatedly directs his or her attention to processes of becoming, flourishing, and blossoming will feel something faintly resembling the sensation we experience as we watch the sun rise. Processes of withering and dying, on the other hand, will produce an experience that may be compared with what we feel as we watch the slow rise of the moon on the horizon.

Cultivated appropriately and trained in ever livelier and more active fashion, these two types of feeling become forces that can lead to the most significant spiritual effects. Deliberately, regularly, and repeatedly surrendering to such feelings, we find a new world opening before us. The soul world or so-called astral plane begins to dawn. Growth and decay are now no longer merely facts, evoking vague impressions, as they were before. Instead, they form definite spiritual lines and figures we had no inkling of before. What is more, these lines and figures change their forms with the phenomena. A blossoming flower conjures up a particular line before our souls, while a growing animal or a dying tree gives rise to other lines. In this way, the soul world (or astral plane) spreads out before us.

These lines and figures are not arbitrary. Two students at the same level of development will see the same lines and figures associated with the same processes. Just as two healthy people with good eyes both see a round table as round—and neither sees it as rectangular—so, in the presence of a flower, two souls both see the same spiritual form arising. Just as biologists customarily describe and classify plants and animals according to their forms (which are the same for every observer), so experts in spiritual science describe and characterize the spiritual forms of the processes of growth and death and distinguish various species and types among them.

6. Once we have advanced to the point where we can see the spiritual forms of what appears physically visible to our outer eyes, then we are not far from the stage of seeing things that have no physical existence at all. Such things, of course, remain completely hidden (or occult) to one who has received no esoteric training.

7. Here it must be emphasized that the spiritual researchers should not lose themselves in reflection upon what this or that might mean. Mental activity of this kind will only lead us astray. We should look out at the world with healthy, alert senses and a keen power of observation,

and then give ourselves over to our feelings. We should not try to determine what things mean with the speculative mind, but should let things themselves tell us their meaning.[1]

8. Another important point is what esoteric science calls "orientation" in the higher worlds. We achieve such an orientation when we have filled ourselves completely with the consciousness that feelings and thoughts are actual facts, just as real as tables and chairs are in the physical-sensory world. In the worlds of soul and thought, feelings and thoughts affect one another just as sensory things do in the physical world. Until we are actively filled with the consciousness of the reality of thoughts and feelings, we cannot believe that entertaining a wrong thought can have as devastating an effect on the other thoughts that animate our thought world as a bullet shot blindly from a rifle has on things it hits in the physical world. Thus, although we might never allow ourselves to engage in visible actions that we consider meaningless, we nonetheless do not shrink from entertaining wrong thoughts or feelings, because these do not seem to us to be dangerous to the rest of the world.

To move forward on the path to higher knowledge and advance in spiritual science, we must therefore pay as careful attention to our thoughts and feelings as we do to

---

1. It should be noted that artistic feeling or sensitivity, coupled with a quiet, inward nature, is the most promising precondition for developing spiritual faculties. Such artistic sensitivity penetrates through the surface of things and thus reaches their secrets.

our movements in the physical world. For instance, we do not usually try to go straight through a wall, but direct our steps around it; that is, we comply with the laws of the physical world. The world of feelings and thoughts likewise has its own laws, but they do not force themselves upon us from the outside. Rather, they must flow out of the life of the soul.

For this to occur, we must never allow ourselves false thoughts and feelings. Random musings, playful daydreams, the arbitrary ebb and flow of feeling—all these must be banished from the soul. We need not fear that this will make us unfeeling. On the contrary, we will find that only when we regulate our inner life in this way do we become truly rich in feelings and creative in genuine imagination. Important feelings and fruitful thoughts will then take the place of petty indulgence in emotions and the playful association of ideas. These, in turn, will help us to orient ourselves in the spiritual world, thereby allowing us to enter into a right relationship with the things in it. And this, too, has a definite, noticeable effect.

Just as we find our way as physical beings among the things of the physical world, so now our path leads us through the phenomena of growing and dying away, as we come to know these in the manner described above. We follow the processes of growing and flourishing, decaying and dying, just as our own and the world's development require.

9. The students of occult knowledge must also direct their attention to the world of *sounds*. Here we must

distinguish between sounds produced by so-called inanimate objects (such as a falling object, a bell, or a musical instrument) and those coming from living beings (animals or human beings). If we hear a bell, we perceive the sound and associate it with a pleasant feeling. The scream of an animal, on the other hand, not only evokes an emotional association but also reveals the animal's inner experience, its pleasure or its pain. In esoteric training, we focus on the second type of sound, concentrating our whole attention on the fact that the sound communicates something that lies outside our own souls.

We must immerse ourselves in this "otherness," inwardly uniting our feelings with the pain or pleasure expressed by the sound. To do this, we must disregard what the sound is *for us*—whether it is pleasant or unpleasant, agreeable or disagreeable. Our soul must be filled only with what is happening in the being from whom the sound comes. If we practice this exercise systematically and deliberately, we will acquire as we do so the faculty of merging, as it were, with the being that made the sound. A musically sensitive person will naturally find this particular exercise for the cultivation of soul life easier than one who is unmusical. But no one should think that a musical ear is a substitute for systematically doing the exercise. As occult students, our goal is to learn to feel toward the whole of nature in this way.

As we learn to do so, a new faculty takes root in the world of feeling and thought. All of nature begins to whisper its secrets to us through its sounds. Sounds that were previously incomprehensible to our soul now become the meaningful language of nature. Where we had heard only noise in the sounds produced by inanimate objects, we now learn a new language of the soul. As this cultivation of our feelings continues, we become aware that we can hear things we never conceived of before; indeed, we begin to hear with our souls.

10. Something must be added to this practice before the highest point in this region of soul experience can be attained. Particularly important as we develop as occult pupils is that we also work on the way we listen to other people when they speak. On the path to higher knowledge this listening skill is extremely important. We must become accustomed to listening in such a way that we quiet our own inner life completely when we listen. For example, when someone expresses an opinion and another listens, agreement or disagreement usually stirs immediately within the listener. Often in such a situation we feel compelled to express our own opinion at once, especially if we disagree. However, on the path to higher knowledge we must learn to silence any agreement or disagreement with the opinions we hear. Naturally, this does not mean that we should suddenly change our way of life and strive to achieve this complete inner silence all the time. We must start with isolated instances that we choose intentionally. Then quite slowly and gradually, as if by itself, this new way of listening will become a habit.

In spiritual research, we practice this new way of listening in a systematic way. As students, we should feel it our duty to set aside, as an exercise, certain times when we listen to the most contrary opinions, completely silencing within us all agreement and, especially, all negative judgments. Not only must we silence our intellectual judgment but also any feelings of disapproval, rejection, or even agreement. Above all, we must observe ourselves carefully to ensure that such feelings, even though absent from the surface of the soul, are not present in its innermost depths. For example, we must learn to listen to the remarks of those who are in some way inferior to us, suppressing *every* feeling of superiority or knowing better.

Listening to children in this way is especially useful, and even the wisest of us can learn a great deal from them. These exercises teach us to listen selflessly to the words of others, completely excluding our own personality, opinions, and feelings. Once we are practiced in listening in this way without criticism, then gradually, even when the most contradictory views and illogical statements are aired before us, we begin to learn how to unite ourselves with the being of the other person and fully enter into it. We begin to hear through the words, into the other person's soul. As we consistently practice this new habit, sound becomes the medium through which we can perceive soul and spirit.

This practice requires the strictest self-discipline, but it also leads to a lofty goal. For when the exercise is combined with those given above in connection with sounds in nature, then a new sense of hearing comes to life in the soul. The soul becomes capable of hearing "words" from the spiritual world that are not expressed in outer tones and cannot be heard by physical ears. Perception of the "inner word" awakens. Truths are gradually revealed to us out of the spiritual world. We hear ourselves spoken to spiritually.[2]

All higher truths are attained only through such inward prompting. Whatever we hear from the lips of true spiritual researchers is only what they have brought into experience in this way. This does not mean that it is unnecessary to study esoteric literature before we ourselves have become able to hear this "inner word." On the contrary, reading such writings and listening to the teachings of esoteric researchers are themselves a means of achieving knowledge for ourselves. Indeed, every statement of spiritual science that we hear is intended to guide the mind in the direction it must take if the soul is to experience any true progress. Therefore the exercises described here should be accompanied by the intensive study of what researchers in spiritual science bring into the world. Such study is part of the preparatory work in all schools of esoteric training.

In fact, all the other methods taken together will not get us anywhere if we do not also absorb the teachings of esoteric researchers. These teachings are drawn forth from the living "inner word," from "living inspiration," and therefore they themselves are spiritually alive. They are not just words. They are living forces. And as we follow

---

2. Only when we have learned to listen selflessly and to be inwardly receptive, without any personal opinion or feeling stirring in us, can the higher beings described by spiritual science speak to us. The beings of the spiritual world will remain silent as long as we still pit any personal feelings or opinions against what we hear from others.

the words of one experienced in esoteric knowledge or read a book based on true inner experience, forces are at work in our souls that make us seers (clairvoyants), just as the forces of nature have shaped our eyes and ears out of living matter.

Illumination

11. The stage of illumination starts from very simple processes. Here, too, as in the stage of preparation, it is a matter of developing and awakening certain feelings and thoughts latent in every one of us. Anyone who focuses on these simple processes with persistence, rigor, and complete patience will be led to a perception of the inner manifestations of light.

We begin by examining different natural objects in a particular way: for example, a transparent, beautifully shaped stone (a crystal), a plant, and an animal. First, we try to direct our whole attention to comparing a stone and an animal. The thoughts that we form to make this comparison must pass through the soul accompanied by lively *feelings*. No other thoughts or feelings must be allowed to intrude and disturb our intense, attention-filled observation. We should say to ourselves: "The stone has a form. The animal also has a form. The stone stays peacefully in its place. The animal changes its place. It is instinct (or desire) that moves the animal to change its place. Instincts are also served by the animal's form. Its organs and limbs are shaped by these instincts. Stones, on the other hand, are not shaped by desires, but rather by a force that is without desire."[3]

As we immerse ourselves intensely in these thoughts, observing stone and animal with close attention, two very different kinds of feeling come to life in the soul. One kind streams into the soul from the stone, another from the animal. Although this exercise will probably not succeed in the beginning, gradually, if we practice with real patience, the two feelings will eventually appear. We need only practice the exercise over and over again. At first, the feelings persist only as long as the observation lasts. Later, they continue to work on after the exercise is over. Eventually, they become something that remains alive in our souls. At that point, we need only to reflect for stone and animal feelings to arise again, even without the contemplation of an external object. Out of these feelings, and the thoughts accompanying them, organs of clairvoyance are formed.

If we add plants to our observations, we notice that the feeling streaming from a plant, both in its nature and intensity, lies midway between what streams from a stone and what streams from an animal. The organs built up in this way are *spiritual eyes*. They gradually allow us to see soul and spiritual colors. But as long as we have not made our own what was previously described as the path or stage of

---

3. The above-mentioned facts concerning the contemplation of crystals have been distorted and misrepresented by people who have only superficial (exoteric) knowledge of them. This has led to notions of "crystal-gazing," and so on. Such distortions are based on misunderstandings. Although they have been described in many books, they are in no way a subject of true (esoteric) spiritual teaching.

"preparation," the lines and figures of the spiritual world remain dark. Through the process of illumination, they become light. Here again it must be noted that the words used, such as *dark* and *light*, as well as other expressions, are only approximations of what is meant. Our ordinary languages were created for physical relationships. If we use ordinary language, as we must, only approximations of spiritual phenomena are possible.

Thus occult science describes what clairvoyant organs perceive as flowing from stones as "blue" or "blue-red," while what flows from animals is described as "red" or "red-yellow." In fact, the colors seen are "spiritual" colors. The color streaming from plants is "green," gradually fading into a light, etheric rose-pink. Plants are actually the only natural beings whose constitution in the higher worlds resembles to some extent their constitution in the physical world. This is not the case with stones or animals.

Obviously, the above-mentioned colors represent only the main tones of the mineral, animal, and plant kingdoms; in reality all possible intermediary hues exist. Each stone, plant, and animal has its own particular color nuance. To this picture must be added the beings of the higher worlds that never incarnate physically; their colors can be magnificent, but sometimes they are horrible. On the whole, the range of color in the higher worlds is immeasurably greater than in the physical world.

12. Once we achieve the capacity of seeing with "spiritual eyes," we sooner or later meet the higher beings mentioned above, as well as sometimes also those beings, lower than we, who never enter our physical reality.

13. Having brought our practice to the point described here, paths to many worlds lie open before us. But no one is advised to proceed further without paying careful attention to what is said or communicated by spiritual researchers. In fact, even with regard to what has already been said, it is always best to heed experienced guidance. Naturally, if we have the strength and persistence to reach these elementary levels of illumination, we will certainly seek and find the right kind of direction.

14. One precaution, at all events, is essential, and whoever is unwilling to adopt it had better not proceed in occult science at all. As esoteric students, we must not lose any of our human qualities but must remain noble-minded, good people, sensitive to all aspects of physical reality. In fact, throughout the course of our esoteric training, we must continuously increase our moral strength, inner integrity, and faculty of observation. During the basic exercises, for example, we must seek to enlarge not only our compassion for the human and animal worlds but also our sense for the beauty of nature. If we do not bear this in mind, then both these feelings and our aesthetic sense will be dulled by the exercises. Our heart will become hard, our senses blunted. Clearly, this would have dangerous consequences.

15. What happens in the stage of illumination after we have practiced the stone, plant, and animal exercises and have risen to a consideration of the human being, and how, after illumination, the soul unites with the spiritual world under all circumstances and so is led to initiation— all this, the next sections will describe, insofar as it is possible to do so.

16. Many people today seek a path to occult or esoteric science. Their quest takes various forms. Many dangerous, and even illicit, practices are tried. Therefore those who believe that they know something of the truth in these matters should give others the opportunity to learn something about esoteric training. This book presents such an opportunity, nothing more. Something of the truth must be made known to prevent error from causing great harm. No harm will come to anyone on this path, provided he or she does not seek to force results.

Just one thing must be borne in mind: we should not spend more time and energy on these exercises than is in keeping with our position and duties in life. Pursuing a path of esoteric training should never lead to any sudden change in one's life situation. If we want real results, we must have patience. We must be able to stop the exercises after just a few minutes and continue with our daily work as usual. We must not let thoughts of our exercises mingle with our work. Whoever has not learned to wait, in the noblest and best sense of the word, is unsuited to esoteric work and will never achieve results of any real value.

Controlling our Thoughts and Feelings

17. As we seek esoteric knowledge on the path described above, one thought can give us strength in all our efforts. We must never forget that we may already have advanced quite far, even though this progress has not manifested in ways we might expect. If we do not remember this, we can easily lose heart and give up our efforts

completely. In the beginning, the forces and capacities that we must develop are extremely delicate. Their nature is quite other than we previously imagined. Until now we have been used to dealing only with the physical world. The realms of soul and spirit had escaped our vision and our grasp. Thus it is not surprising that we do not notice immediately that forces of soul and spirit are beginning to develop in us.

There is the possibility of error here for anyone who undertakes an esoteric path while remaining ignorant of the experiences gathered by accomplished spiritual researchers. Such spiritual researchers can see our progress long before we are aware of it. They know that delicate spiritual eyes can develop before we are aware of them. Indeed, the instructions of researchers are for the most part designed to keep us from losing our confidence, patience, and perseverance at a time when we cannot yet see our progress for ourselves.

Esoteric teachers cannot give us anything that is not already present, although concealed, within us. They can only guide us in the development of our own dormant capacities. Nevertheless, what they communicate out of their experience will be a help to us when we seek to struggle from the darkness into the light.

18. Many people abandon the path to occult knowledge soon after embarking upon it because they do not notice any immediate progress. Students often mistake their first perceptible higher experiences for illusions when these do not correspond with what they had expected. Such students lose courage because they consider their first experiences

worthless or because these experiences seem insignificant and unlikely to lead to anything more valuable in the foreseeable future. *Courage* and *self-confidence* are two beacons that should never be extinguished on the path to higher knowledge. No one, who cannot patiently repeat an exercise that has failed, to all appearances, countless times before, will travel far on this path.

19. Long before we have a clear perception of our progress, we have a vague feeling that we are on the right track. This feeling should be cultivated and nurtured, for it can become a reliable guide. Above all, we must eradicate the belief that only bizarre and mysterious practices lead to higher knowledge. We should be clear that development begins with the feelings and thoughts we live with all the time, but that these feelings and thoughts must be given a new, unaccustomed direction. We must say to ourselves: "Within my own feelings and thoughts the highest mysteries lie concealed, but until now I have not perceived them." In the final analysis, everything is based on the simple fact that, though we carry body, soul, and spirit about with us, we are *conscious* only of the body. The esoteric student must become as conscious of soul and spirit as the ordinary person is of his or her body.

20. It all comes down to giving our feelings and thoughts the right direction. Only then can we gain the ability to see what ordinarily remains invisible. One of the ways of achieving this will be given here. Once again, it is a simple exercise, like almost everything that has been presented so far. Yet the effects of this exercise, if carried

out with perseverance, devotion, and the necessary inner mood, will be far-reaching.

21. We place before us a small seed from a plant. Starting with this insignificant thing, the point will be to think the right thoughts intensively, and by means of these thoughts to develop certain feelings. First, we must establish what we are really seeing with our eyes. We describe to ourselves the form, color, and other properties of the seed. Then we ponder the thought: "This seed, if planted in the ground, will grow into a complex plant." We visualize the plant, we make it present to and in us. We build it up in imagination. Then we think: "What I now visualize in my imagination, forces of earth and light will later in reality draw forth from this small seed. But if this were an artificial seed, an artificial copy so perfect that my eyes could not distinguish it from a real seed, then no forces of earth and light would ever be able to draw forth such a plant from it." If we can clearly form this thought and bring it to life within us, then we will be able to form the next thought easily and with the right feeling: "Within the seed already lies concealed what—as the force of the whole plant—later grows out of it. The artificial copy of the seed has no such force. Yet, to my eyes, both seeds look the same. Therefore the real seed contains something invisible that is absent in the copy." [4]

---

4. To object here that a microscopic examination would reveal the differences between the real seed and the artificial copy is to admit that one has not understood what is at issue here. The point is not to determine what exactly we are looking at, but to develop soul-spiritual forces.

Thoughts and feelings should now focus on this invisible reality. We must imagine that this invisible force or reality will in the course of time change into the visible plant, whose color and form we will be able to see before us. We should hold the thought: "The invisible will become visible. If I were unable to think, then what later becomes visible could not announce itself to me now."

22. It is important to emphasize that whatever we think we must also feel with intensity. Meditative thoughts need to be experienced calmly and peacefully. No other thoughts should distract us. Time should be allowed for both the thought, and the feeling united with it, to penetrate the soul. If this is done in the right way, then after a time—perhaps only after many unsuccessful attempts—we become conscious of a new force within us. This creates a new perception. The seed seems to be enclosed in a small cloud of light. In a sensory-spiritual way, we sense it as a kind of flame. At its center, we experience a sensation similar to the impression made by the color purple, at its edges a sensation similar to the color blue.

What we could not see before now becomes apparent to us, created by the force of the thoughts and feelings that we have awakened within us. The plant—which is still physically invisible and will not become visible until later—is revealed to us in a spiritually visible manner.

23. Understandably, some people consider all this mere illusion. Many will say, "I do not want to have anything to do with such hallucinations and visions." Some will fall away and abandon the path. What it comes down

to is this: fantasy and spiritual reality must not be confused in this complex matter of inner development. We must have the courage to push forward and not become faint-hearted and fearful. On the other hand, we must always cultivate a healthy sense for the distinction between truth and illusion. We should never lose conscious self-control during the exercises. Our thinking must be as certain and reliable in carrying out the exercises as it is when we apply it to the things and processes of everyday life.

We must remain clear-headed and down-to-earth at all times. It would be very bad indeed if we fell into daydreaming. Our reasoning must be perfectly lucid, even sober, at all times. The greatest mistake would be to lose our equilibrium through such exercises, and thus be hindered from forming as sound and sensible opinions in everyday life as we did before. Therefore, we should examine ourselves repeatedly to ensure that we have not lost our balance, and that we still remain the same within the relationships of our daily lives as we were before we started the exercises.

Steady inner calm, and a clear mind for all things—these must be preserved. Above all, we must take care not to indulge each passing reverie or give ourselves up to every possible different kind of exercise. The directions for thinking given here have been tested and practiced in occult schools from the most ancient times. Only such time-tested methods are presented here. To use other methods, either ones we have created ourselves or those we have read or heard about, will lead inevitably to a path of error and boundless fantasy.

24. A further exercise, connected to the seed meditation, is the following. We place before us a mature plant. First, we immerse ourselves in the thought: "A time will come when this plant will wither and decay. Everything I see now will then no longer exist. But the plant will have produced seeds, and these will become new plants. Thus once again I become aware that something I cannot see lies hidden in what I can see." We saturate ourselves with the thought: "The plant form with all its colors will soon no longer be there. But the knowledge that the plant produces seeds teaches me that it will not disappear into nothingness. I cannot see what preserves the plant from disappearance anymore than I could see the future plant in the seed. Therefore it follows that there is something in the plant, too, that I cannot see with my eyes. But if I let this thought live within me, and the appropriate feeling unites with it, then after a time new force will grow in my soul and become a new perception." A kind of spiritual flame form will then grow out of the plant. Of course, this flame will be correspondingly larger than the one described in the case of the seed. It will be felt as green-blue at its center and as yellow-red at its periphery.

25. Again, it must be strongly emphasized that we do *not* see what are here called "colors" in the same way that we see colors with our physical eyes. Rather, through spiritual perception we experience something similar to the impression made by physical colors. To perceive "blue" spiritually is to feel or sense an impression similar to the one we feel when our physical eyes dwell on the color blue. We must remember this if

we wish to ascend gradually to true spiritual perception. If we do not, we will expect the spiritual world to be a replica of the physical world, which would confuse us in the worst way.

26. Once we have reached the point of such spiritual seeing, we have already achieved much. Things now reveal to us not only their present being but also their arising and passing away. We begin to see the spirit—of which our physical eyes know nothing—everywhere. We have begun to approach the mystery of birth and death with our own intuitive vision.

As far as our physical senses are concerned, an entity comes into being with birth and passes away with death. But this is only because the outer senses cannot perceive the hidden spirit. For the spirit, birth and death are merely transformations, just as the burgeoning of a bud into a blossom is a transformation occurring before our physical eyes. To come to know this firsthand through our own spiritual vision, we must first awaken spiritual senses for it in the way indicated here.

27. Those who have had some soul (or psychic) experience of the supersensible worlds might object that there are shorter and simpler ways to attain spiritual perception. Indeed, it cannot be disputed that some people come to know the phenomena of birth and death through personal vision without undertaking the exercises described here. Some people have considerable psychic gifts, which require only slight stimulation in order to be developed further. But such people are exceptional. The path described here is safer and more generally effective.

A person may achieve some knowledge of chemistry in unusual ways, but if we wish to become real chemists, we must follow the more certain and generally accepted path.

28. We would be committing a serious error, with far-reaching consequences, if we believed that we could reach our objective more easily by dispensing with the actual object of our meditation and simply forming a mental picture of the seed (or plant) that we then held in our imaginations. This path may indeed also lead us to results, but it is not as sure and proven as the one presented in this book. For the perceptions we attain in this way often turn out to be delusions of fantasy—and we must then wait for these to be transformed into genuine spiritual vision. The point of these exercises is not that we arbitrarily create perceptions for ourselves but that reality creates them in us. The truth must well up from the depths of our own souls—but the ordinary I should not be the magician who conjures up the truth. The beings whose spiritual truth I seek to behold must conjure their own truth.

29. When, by practicing such exercises, we have discovered in ourselves the first rudiments of spiritual perception, we can then go on to contemplate our fellow human beings. We begin by selecting some simple phenomena connected with human life. But before we take this step, we must work sincerely and seriously on the integrity of our moral character. We must remove all thoughts of ever using the knowledge gained in this way for our own self-interest. We must firmly decide never to use for evil ends any power we might gain over other

people. Thus, if we seek to penetrate the mysteries of human nature through our own efforts, we must abide by the golden rule of the occult sciences. This rule states: "For every single step that you take in seeking knowledge of hidden truths, you must take three steps in perfecting your character toward the good." Whoever follows this rule can do the following exercises.

30. We visualize a person whom we have observed longing for something, and we direct our attention to this desire. It is best to recall the moment when the desire was strongest, and we did not yet know whether the person would obtain the object of their desire. Then we surrender ourselves to this picture, completely dedicated to what we can observe in our memory. We create the greatest imaginable inner calm in our souls. We try as far as possible to be deaf and blind to everything else going on around us. Above all, we pay close attention to any feeling that the mental image we have formed awakens in our souls. Then we allow this feeling to rise up within us, like a cloud on an otherwise empty horizon.

Naturally, this exercise often breaks down. We find that we were usually unable to observe the person who is the object of our attention in a state of desire for a sufficient length of time. The lack of firsthand observation interferes with our contemplation and cuts it short. Thus we may have to make hundreds upon hundreds of unsuccessful attempts. Above all, we must not lose patience.

Eventually, after many attempts, we shall experience in ourselves a feeling corresponding to the inner soul state of the individual we are contemplating. Then, before long, we begin to notice that this feeling produces a force in the soul. This force then becomes the spiritual perception of the other person's soul state. An image, experienced as shining, enters our field of vision. This spiritual, shining picture is the so-called astral embodiment of the state of soul we observed—that is, of the desire. As before, we perceive this as flame-like; its center gives an impression of the color yellow-red, and its periphery affects us as the color red-blue or purple would.

It is important that we handle these spiritual perceptions gently. It is best, to begin with, not to talk about them, except perhaps with our teacher if we have one. If we try to describe such a phenomenon in inappropriate language, it usually leads to gross delusions. Ordinary words were not made for such things and are too coarse and clumsy to do them justice. The result is that when we attempt to describe our experience in such words, we are misled into mixing all kinds of fantastic illusions with real spiritual visions.

Here, then, is another important rule for the student of occult knowledge: "Know how to be silent about your spiritual perceptions. Yes, even be silent about them with yourself. Do not try to clothe in words what you see in the spirit, nor try to understand it with your ordinary, unskilled reason. Give yourself fully to your spiritual perception, and do not disturb it with too much pondering. Remember that your thinking is not yet on the level of your spiritual vision. You have acquired this thinking in a life that until now has been limited wholly to the physical world. But what you are now acquiring goes beyond that. Therefore do not seek to measure these new, higher perceptions by the same standard that you measured your old ones."

Once we can observe our inner experiences steadily, then we can speak about them and thereby inspire our fellow human beings to activity.

31. The above exercise may be supplemented by the following complementary one. This time we contemplate a person whose desire or longing has been fulfilled. Following the same rules and precautions as before, we attain another, different spiritual perception. We again see a spiritual flame-form, but now this feels yellow in the center and light green at the periphery.

32. Observing and contemplating our fellow human beings in this way, we can easily fall into a moral error. We can lose our love for them. We must do everything imaginable to ensure that this does not happen. In fact, we should undertake these exercises only when we have developed the absolute certainty that thoughts are realities. Then we shall not allow ourselves to think of our fellow human beings in any way that is incompatible with the profound respect due their dignity and freedom. The idea that another person could be merely an object of observation must never, even for a moment, take hold of us.

Every esoteric observation of human nature must be accompanied by self-education in the ability to appreciate unreservedly the full individual value of every person. All that dwells within each human being, including thoughts and feelings, must be considered holy and inviolable. We must be filled with a profound awe for everything human, even in our memories and recollections.

33. These preliminary exercises give two examples of how we may gain insight into human nature. If nothing else, they show the path that we must follow. Indeed, we need only discover the necessary inner quiet and calm belonging to such meditations for our souls to undergo a great transformation. The inner enrichment that we experience in our being soon makes even our outer conduct more confident and serene. And this transformed behavior then reacts positively upon our souls. Thereby we help ourselves along in our development.

We will always find ways and means of discovering more and more of human nature that is hidden from our outer senses. As we do so, we gradually progress to the point of glimpsing the mysterious kinship between human nature and all else that exists in the universe. In this way, we shall be drawing closer to the moment when we can take the first steps in the stage of initiation.

But before we can take these first steps, one thing more is necessary, though to begin with we cannot see why this is so. Later, however, we shall understand it.

34. Candidates for initiation must bring with them two additional qualities: courage and fearlessness. These have a certain relationship with each other and must be developed together. As esoteric students, we must deliberately seek out situations in which these virtues may be cultivated. Indeed, in occult training they are developed quite systematically. From this point of view, life itself is also a good occult school—perhaps the best. We must be able to look danger calmly in the eye and overcome difficulties without hesitation. When facing a danger, we should

immediately be stirred to the conviction: "All fear is use-less. I must not let it take hold of me. I must think only of what is to be done." In fact, we must reach a point, in situations that earlier would have caused us to be afraid, in which the very idea of *fear* and *lack of courage* become things impossible for us to conceive in the core of our soul.

Such self-education in courage and fearlessness develops quite specific forces that we need for initiation into higher knowledge. Just as we need healthy nerves as physical beings to make use of our physical senses, so—as beings of soul—we need the strength that develops only in courageous and fearless natures. For as we penetrate the higher mysteries, we see things that were previously hidden from us by the illusions of the senses. In fact, it is a blessing that our physical senses do not allow us to perceive the higher truths. In this way they protect us from things that, if we saw them unprepared, would cause us great dismay, things we could not bear to see. As students of the occult, we must train ourselves to bear these sights. In the process, we shall inevitably lose some of the supports that the external world provided for us as long as we were caught up in its illusions. What happens is literally the same as when people are made aware of a danger that was present for a long time, but which they knew nothing of. Unaware of the danger, they were of course also unafraid. But once they know about it, they are overcome with fear—even though the danger has not increased by their knowing about it.

35. The world's powers are both destructive and constructive; the fate of sense-perceptible beings is to arise

and pass away. The initiate must see and understand how these forces and this fate work themselves out. For this, the veil that lies before our spiritual eyes in ordinary life must be removed. Of course, we ourselves are closely interwoven with these forces and with fate. Our individual natures, like the world, contain destructive and constructive forces. As initiates, our own souls will be revealed before our seeing eyes as nakedly as all other things.

Students must not lose strength in the face of such self-knowledge. They must come to meet it with a surplus of forces. In order to have this surplus, we must learn to maintain our inward calm and certainty in difficult life situations and cultivate an unshakable trust in the good powers of existence. We should be prepared for the fact that many motives that have previously guided us can no longer do so. We shall have to realize that we thought and did many things simply because we were caught up in ignorance. The grounds we had for doing things no longer hold good. We may often have acted out of conceit, but we now come to realize how unspeakably useless all vanity is to the initiate. We have been motivated by greed; now we realize how destructive greed is. We have to develop completely new grounds for acting and thinking. This is what involves courage and fearlessness.

36. Above all, we need to cultivate courage and fearlessness in the inmost depths of our thought life itself. We must learn not to be discouraged by failure. We should be able to think: "I will forget that I have failed again, and will try once more as if it never happened." In this way we struggle to the conviction that the sources of strength in

the world that we can draw from are inexhaustible. Again and again we aspire to the spirit, which will lift us up and carry us, regardless of how often our earthly being proves to be weak and powerless. We must become capable of living into the future and not let any past experiences disturb our striving.

Once we have developed the above-described qualities to a certain extent, we are ready to learn the *true names* of things. These names are the keys to higher knowledge. Initiation is learning to call the things of the world by the names they have in the minds of their divine authors. These names contain the secrets of things. Initiates speak a different language from the uninitiated because, as initiates, they call things by the names through which they were created. To the extent that initiation can be talked about at all, it will be discussed in the next chapter.

CHAPTER 3

INITIATION

1. Initiation is the highest level of esoteric training about which generally intelligible written indications may still be given. Whatever lies beyond initiation is difficult to communicate in an understandable way. Yet the path to this knowledge is open to all who have worked their way through the stages of preparation, illumination, and initiation and reached the lower mysteries.

2. Initiation bestows upon us knowledge and abilities we would otherwise acquire in a different way and form only in the distant future, after many incarnations. A person initiated today experiences in this life something that he or she would normally experience only later, and under quite different circumstances.

3. We can fully experience only as much of the mysteries of existence as the level of our maturity allows. This is the only reason why we find obstacles on our path to higher knowledge and capacities. One should not use a firearm until one has had enough experience to

use it without causing damage. If we were initiated to-day, without preparation, we would lack the experiences we would otherwise continue to gather through future incarnations up to the moment when, as part of the normal course of our development, these mysteries were revealed to us. As we arrive at the doorway to initiation, these experiences must be replaced by something else.

Therefore the first instructions given to candidates for initiation form a substitute for future experiences they would have had in lives to come. These instructions concern the so-called "trials" through which a candidate must pass. The trials themselves arise as the natural consequence of our soul life when the exercises described in the previous chapters have been practiced in the right way.

4. Such "trials," of course, are often mentioned in books. But by their very nature such descriptions generally give a false impression. For a person who has not passed through the stages of preparation and illumination has never experienced these trials, and therefore cannot correctly describe them.

5. Certain things and facts belonging to the higher worlds necessarily arise for candidates for initiation. But we shall only see and hear these if we are sensitive to the spiritual perception of shapes, colors, sounds, and so forth described in the chapters on preparation and illumination.

6. The first trial consists in achieving a truer perception than the average person possesses of the physical properties, initially of inanimate bodies, and then of plants, animals, and human beings. This has nothing to do with what

is called "scientific knowledge." We are not concerned here with science, but with "perception." As a rule, the procedure is one in which, as candidates for initiation, we learn to recognize how natural things and living beings reveal themselves to our spiritual ears and eyes. In a certain sense, these things stand before us unveiled—or naked. The qualities that we come to see and hear were veiled from our physical sight and hearing. The fact that during initiation this veil falls away is due to a process called "the process of spiritual burning away." For this reason, the first trial is called the *Fire Trial.*

7. For many people, ordinary life itself is already a more or less unconscious process of initiation through the fire trial. Such people have lived a life so rich in experiences that their self-confidence, courage, and steadfastness have matured in healthy ways; they have learned to bear suffering, disappointment, and failure calmly, magnanimously, and with unbroken strength. People who have worked through their experiences in this way are often already, although without knowing it clearly, initiates. It then takes only a little to open their spiritual eyes and ears so that they become seers.

One thing is certain: the purpose of the real fire trial is not to satisfy our curiosity. To be sure, we shall come to know extraordinary facts that other people have no inkling of. But acquaintance with such facts is not the objective; it is but the means to an end. The objective is to acquire truer self-confidence, greater courage, and quite a different kind of magnanimity and endurance than is normally attainable within the lower world.

[handwritten marginalia: "after the 'fire trial' the occult writing is unveiled"]

8. Candidates may still turn back after the fire trial. They may return to ordinary life, strengthened in body and soul, and continue their initiation in a future incarnation. If we decide to do this, we become more useful members of society and humanity in our present incarnation than we were before. Whatever our situation may be, our inner strength, mindfulness, and positive effect on other people will have increased.

9. If, having completed the "fire trial," we decide to continue the path of initiation, then a particular system of writing, customarily used in occult training, is unveiled to us. The characters of this script reveal the actual secret teachings. For what is really "hidden" (or occult) in things is not directly expressible in the words of ordinary language, nor recordable in any ordinary system of writing. Rather, those who have learned from initiates translate the teachings of esoteric science into ordinary language as best they can.

This occult script is inscribed forever in the spiritual world. Once the soul has attained spiritual perception, the script is revealed to it. But we do not learn to read this occult alphabet in the same way that we learn to read an ordinary human alphabet. Rather, it is as if we grow toward clairvoyant knowing, and while we grow, there develops in us—as a soul faculty—a force impelling us to decipher, as if they were the characters of a script, the events and beings of the spiritual world present before us. As our inner development unfolds, it can happen that this power, and the experience of the trial connected with it, appear on their own. However, we shall be more likely to reach our goal if we follow the instructions of experienced esoteric researchers, who are proficient in deciphering the hidden script.

10. The signs of this occult writing are not arbitrarily devised but correspond to the forces at work in the world. Through these signs we learn the language of things. As candidates for initiation we realize immediately that these signs correspond to the figures, colors, and sounds that we learned to perceive in the earlier stages of preparation and illumination. It becomes apparent that all that came before was like learning the letters of the alphabet in order to spell. But now we begin to *read* in the higher world. All that previously appeared only in isolated figures, sounds, and colors now appears as one great connected and interrelated whole. For the first time we experience complete certainty in our observation of the higher worlds. Before, we could never be sure whether the things we saw were seen correctly.

At this point, for the first time, regular communication is possible between candidates and initiates concerning the realms of higher knowledge. For, however closely an initiate may live together with other people in everyday life, he or she can communicate higher knowledge directly only in the sign language mentioned above.

11. Through this language we are introduced to certain rules for the conduct of life. We learn of duties we knew nothing about before. Knowing these rules of conduct, we become able to perform actions with a significance that the actions of uninitiated people could never have. We act out of the higher worlds. The directives for such actions can be received only in the occult script.

12. It should be emphasized that there are people who perform such actions unconsciously, without having undergone an esoteric training. These "helpers of the world and humanity" pass through life bestowing blessings and good deeds wherever they go. For reasons that will not be discussed here, they have been endowed with gifts that seem supernatural. They differ from those following the path to higher knowledge only in that the latter act consciously, understanding the larger context of their actions. What we, as occult students, achieve through training and esoteric practice, the higher powers bestow on these blessed people for the benefit of the whole world. We should revere those so favored by God, but we should not therefore consider the work of esoteric training superfluous.

13. After we have learned to read the occult sign-writing, another "trial" begins. In this trial we must demonstrate that we can move freely and surely in the higher worlds. In ordinary life, impulses from the external world prompt our actions. We work at this or that job because our situation imposes certain duties upon us. Needless to say, we must not neglect any of our duties because we are living in the higher worlds. No higher duty should force us to neglect even one of our duties in the ordinary world. If we are parents, we shall continue to fulfill our responsibilities just as well as we did before entering upon the path to higher knowledge. Whatever our job may be, whether government official or soldier, following the path to higher knowledge should not keep us from doing our job. On the contrary, esoteric training enhances, to a

degree inconceivable to the uninitiated, the very qualities
that make us competent in life. If this does not always
seem to be the case, it is because those who have not been
initiated do not know how to judge those who have been.
The actions of the initiated are not always readily compre-
hensible to others. But, as has been said, this applies in
just a few cases.

14. We have now reached a level of initiation where we
have duties to perform but no outward reason to do so.
We are moved to carry them out not by external circumstances, but only by the standards revealed to us in the
"hidden" language of the secret script. In this second trial
we must demonstrate that we can act according to these
standards as surely and steadily as good secretaries carry
out the duties that devolve upon them. To this end, we
shall feel ourselves faced, in the course of our training,
with a particular task. We must act on the basis of perceptions made as a result of what we learned during preparation and illumination. We must discover what we are to
do by reading the occult writing that we have now made
our own. If we can recognize our duty and carry it out correctly, then we have successfully passed this trial.

We can tell whether we have succeeded in carrying out
a duty from the changes in the figures, colors, and sounds
we perceive with our spiritual ears and eyes. The instructions for esoteric training describe exactly what these figures and so on are supposed to look like after our action,
and how we are to perceive them. As candidates for initiation, we must learn how to produce such changes in our
spiritual perceptions. This trial is called the *Water Trial*

because when we act in these higher realms, outer circumstances no longer "support" us, just as we lose the
ground under our feet when we swim in deep water. This
practice should be repeated until we have complete confidence in our abilities.

15. As in the fire trial, the water trial has to do with acquiring a certain quality or virtue that would normally
take many incarnations to develop. But as a result of our
experiences in the higher world, we are able to develop
this quality in a short time and to an advanced degree. The
point is this: in order to produce these changes in the
higher realms we must learn to act wholly according to
our spiritual perceptions and our reading of the secret
script. If we let any personal wishes, opinions, and so
forth enter this activity—if we fail even for a moment to
comply with the laws we know are right (and follow instead our own whims)—then something quite different
will happen than was intended. Our activity would immediately lose its bearings, its objective, and confusion
would intrude.

This trial provides us with abundant opportunities for
the development of self-control, which is of prime importance. The trial will thus be easier for those who have acquired self-control in their lives before initiation. Those
who can follow high principles and ideals, regardless of
personal feelings and desires—who understand the need
to perform duties even when inclinations and sympathies
turn them in another direction—are already and without
knowing it initiates in ordinary life. For such people, passing this second trial will be an easy matter. Indeed, it must

be said that as a rule one must already have achieved a certain, albeit unconscious, degree of initiation to pass this trial. For just as it is difficult to learn to write as an adult when one has not learned to do so as a child, so it is difficult to develop the self-control necessary at the moment of insight into higher worlds if one has not already achieved a certain amount of self-control in everyday life. Our wishes, desires, and inclinations do not change the realities of the physical world, but they have a real effect on things in the higher worlds. To produce a particular effect in the higher worlds, therefore, we must have complete power over ourselves—we must be able to follow the right discipline and not be subject to our own arbitrariness.

16. An important human quality that enters into consideration above all else at this stage of initiation is an unconditionally sound, reliable power of judgment. This faculty needs to be trained through all the earlier stages. Whether this has been done or not shows whether we are fit for the true path of knowledge. For to continue on this path we must now be able to distinguish true reality from illusion, insubstantial figments of the imagination, superstition, and all manner of delusion. Making this distinction is to begin with more difficult on these higher planes of existence than on the lower ones. All preconceptions and cherished beliefs must disappear; truth alone must be the guiding principle. We have to be perfectly prepared to let go of any thought, opinion, or inclination if logical thinking demands it. Certainty in the higher worlds cannot be attained if one is in any way attached to one's own opinions.

17. Progress on the esoteric path is impossible if our way of thinking tends toward fantasy and superstition. We are on the verge of gaining a precious gift. We are about to lose all doubts concerning the higher worlds. They are to be revealed before our spiritual eyes in all their lawfulness. But we cannot receive this treasure as long as we allow ourselves to be deceived by illusion and delusion. It would be fatal if we allowed fantasy and prejudices to run away with our reason. Indeed, dreamers and fantasists are as little fitted for the occult path as are those who are superstitious. The worst enemies on the path of higher cognition are dreaming, fantasizing, and superstition. These enemies cannot be taken too seriously. Nevertheless, we must always remember that although "All prejudices must fall from you" is inscribed over the door leading to the second trial, and "Without healthy human understanding all steps are in vain" stands at the entrance to the first, this by no means implies that esoteric students lose the poetry of life and the capacity for enthusiasm.

18. Once we have matured sufficiently along these lines, a third trial awaits us. This trial is without any tangible, distinct goal. Everything is up to us. We find ourselves in a situation where nothing moves us to act. We must each find our own way, by ourselves and out of ourselves. There are no things or people who might help us to act. Nothing and nobody can give us the strength we need, except we ourselves. If we do not find this strength within ourselves, we will soon be back where we were before. It must be said, however, that such failures are rare.

Having passed the previous trials, we are likely to find the strength. A person who has not turned back before will generally succeed this time, too.

Here what matters is the ability to collect oneself promptly and act decisively. For now, in the true sense of the word, we must discover the "higher self." We must re-solve at every moment to listen to the inspiration of the spirit in all things. There is no longer time for scruples, doubts, and so on. Each moment of hesitation only proves that we are not yet ready. We must courageously over-come all that keeps us from listening to the spirit. What matters is that we show presence of mind under these cir-cumstances. This is the quality or attribute to be culti-vated during this stage of development. For this purpose, all our habitual enticements to act, and even to think, now disappear. To avoid falling into passivity, therefore, our task is not to lose ourselves. Only within ourselves will we find a fixed point to hold onto. No one who reads these lines without knowing anything about what they refer to should feel any antipathy for this condition of being thrown back upon oneself. On the contrary, to pass this trial means the highest bliss.

19. Everyday life can serve as an esoteric school for spiritual presence of mind, just as it does for the other qualities required for initiation. This is particularly true in the case of those who, suddenly confronted with life tasks or problems, have learned to act rapidly and decisively, without hesitation or reflection. We learn this ability above all in situations whose successful outcome depends upon speedy action. For example, if we can act quickly

when a misfortune threatens—one that could not be averted if we hesitated even for a moment—and if we can make such decisiveness a permanent quality, we have already unconsciously prepared ourselves for the third "trial." This trial is intended to develop absolute presence of mind.

In schools for esoteric training, this trial is called the *Air Trial.* Here we can rely neither on the solid ground of outer motivation, nor on insights gained from the shapes, colors, and so on we came to know in the stages of preparation and illumination. Instead, we must now rely completely upon ourselves.

20. Once we have passed this trial, we may enter the Temple of Higher Cognition (Wisdom). Of this, little more remains to be said: only the barest indications may be given. The task to be accomplished now is often described as having to swear an "oath" never to "betray" the secret teachings. However, the terms "oath" and "betray" are inaccurate and even misleading. There is no question here of an oath in the ordinary sense of the word. Rather, it is a matter of experience. We learn how to apply the secret teachings, how to place them at the service of humanity. Only now do we begin to understand the world properly. What is important is not to conceal and withhold the higher truths but to learn to present them tactfully, appropriately, and in the right way. What we learn to "keep silent" about is something quite different. We now acquire the noble quality of silence with regard to many things that we used to talk about before—and especially with regard to *how* we used to talk about them.

We would be poor initiates if we did not place the mysteries we have experienced at the service of the world as much as possible. The only obstacle to communication in this area is the failure of others to understand what we say. Naturally, the higher mysteries are not suited to aimless talk and chatter. But this is not to "forbid" a person who has reached this stage of development to speak. No one, neither a human nor any other kind of being, will ever impose such an "oath" upon us. We alone are responsible. We must learn to discover within ourselves what is to be done in every situation. The "oath" means nothing more than that we are ready to bear such a responsibility.

21. When we are sufficiently matured for these experiences, we receive what is called symbolically the "potion of oblivion." That is, we are initiated into the secret of action uninterrupted by the lower memory. This is necessary for an initiate, who must always have complete confidence in the immediate present. We must know how to tear down the veils of memory that surround us at every moment of our lives. Otherwise, if I judge today's experiences by those of yesterday, I become subject to many errors. This does not mean that we should deny our prior experiences. On the contrary, as far as possible, they should always be present. But initiates have to be able to judge each new experience on its own merits and let it work upon them, untroubled by the past.

In other words, I must always be ready to receive a new revelation from each and every being and thing. To judge the new on the basis of the old only leads to errors. Yet the memory of past experiences is useful precisely because it enables one to *see* new ones. That is, without a given past experience I might never see the characteristic feature of the things or beings I encounter. Past experiences should help us to see what is new, not to judge it. As initiates we develop quite specific faculties for this. Thereby many things reveal themselves that remain hidden from the uninitiated.

22. The second potion given to initiates is the "potion of memory." This enables one to keep the higher mysteries always present and in mind. Our ordinary memory is insufficient for this. We must become completely one with the higher mysteries. Merely knowing them is not enough. They must become as much a matter of course to us in our daily actions as eating and drinking are to ordinary people. They must become practice, habit, disposition, so that we do not need to think about them in the ordinary sense. They should express themselves through us, flow through us like the vital functions of our organism. In this way, we grow spiritually closer to the level that nature has already brought us to physically.

CHAPTER 4

PRACTICAL
CONSIDERATIONS

1. Educating our feelings, thoughts, and moods in the ways indicated in the sections on preparation, illumination, and initiation, fashions an organization in our soul and our spirit similar to the one produced by nature in the physical body. Without such a training, our soul and spirit remain unstructured masses. In this state, clairvoyant seers perceive them as intertwined, spiralling, cloudlike vortices. These have a dull glow and are generally sensed as reddish and red-brown or red-yellow in color. After esoteric training, however, the vortices display an orderly structure and are seen as shining spiritually in yellow-green or green-blue colors.

We achieve such a regular structure of soul and spirit—and thereby higher knowledge too—when we order our feelings, thoughts, and moods, just as nature orders our bodily functions, enabling us to see, hear, digest, breathe, speak, and so forth. The order we create in this way gradually enables us to breathe and see with the soul, and to hear, speak, and so on, with the spirit.

2. The present chapter will examine in greater detail some *practical* approaches to esoteric development that are part of the higher education of soul and spirit. These practices are such that basically any of us can adopt them, regardless of any other rules we are following. Indeed, anyone who follows these additional suggestions will advance quite far in esoteric science.

3. We must strive especially to train our capacity for patience. Every stirring of impatience paralyzes, even destroys, the higher faculties latent within us. We should not desire or expect to achieve boundless insights into the higher worlds overnight, for then as a rule they will certainly not come to us. Instead, contentment with even our smallest achievement, along with calm and detachment, should increasingly fill our souls.

Certainly, as students, we are understandably impatient to see the results of our efforts. Yet we can achieve nothing until we can master our impatience. On the other hand, merely to fight against impatience in the ordinary ways does no good. It only strengthens it. We would only be deceiving ourselves and our impatience would sink its roots deeper into our souls. Only if we surrender ourselves repeatedly to a particular *thought*, making it completely our own, can we achieve anything. This thought is: "I must do everything I can for the education of my soul and spirit; but I will wait calmly until the higher powers consider me worthy of illumination." Once this thought has become so powerful in us that it has become part of our character, then we are on the right path.

Before long, this new character trait puts its outward signature upon us. Our gaze becomes calm, our eye steady, our movements confident, our decisions definite. Any nervousness we previously felt gradually disappears. At this point, certain apparently insignificant little "rules" must be observed. For example, let us say someone offends us. Previously, before esoteric training, we would have turned our feelings against the offender. Irritation and anger would have bubbled up within us. Now that we are on the path to higher knowledge, however, the thought immediately comes to us: "This insult does not alter my true worth." Then we do what needs to be done, calmly and with detachment rather than out of anger. This does not mean that we simply swallow insults; rather, we should be as calm and confident in responding to insults directed at us as we would be if we acted on behalf of someone else who had been insulted. We must always bear in mind that esoteric learning does not occur through great outer events but rather through quiet, subtle inner changes in our lives of thought and feeling.

4. Patience has the effect of attracting the treasures of higher knowledge. Impatience repels them. Haste and unrest achieve nothing in the higher realms of existence. Above all, longing and craving must be silenced. These are soul qualities in the face of which all higher knowledge shyly retreats. Precious as higher knowledge is, if it is to come to us, we must not long for it. Moreover, if we wish it only for our own ends, we will never attain it.

This requires in the first place that we be honest with ourselves in the depths of the soul. We can no longer have any illusions about ourselves. We must look our own mistakes, weaknesses, and shortcomings in the eye with inner truthfulness. Each time we find an excuse for a weakness, we place an obstacle before us on our upward path. Such obstacles can be removed only by becoming enlightened about ourselves. There is but one way to overcome failings and weaknesses—to see them for what they are, with inner truthfulness. All that lies dormant in the human soul can be awakened. Even intuition and reason can be improved if—calmly and detachedly—we become clear why we are weak in these areas. Such self-knowledge, of course, is difficult. The temptation to deceive oneself is enormous. But if we make a habit of being honest with ourselves, the doors to greater insight open for us.

5. As esoteric students, we must let all curiosity vanish from us. As far as possible, we must lose the habit of asking questions simply to satisfy our own inquisitiveness. We must learn to ask only those questions that serve to perfect our being for the sake of evolution. Neither our delight in learning, nor our devotion to it, should in any way be diminished by this. On the contrary, we should listen with rapt attention to anything that serves this end and seek every opportunity to practice such devotion.

6. Esoteric development requires, above all, the education of our life of wishes and aspirations. This does not mean that we should have no wishes or desires. If we are to attain something, we must first wish for it. And our wishes will always find fulfillment if a special kind of

force lies behind them. This force or power arises from right knowledge. "Do not aspire to something until you know what is right in a given domain." This is one of the golden rules for the student of esotericism. If we are wise, we will first learn to understand the laws of the world. Then our wishes will become forces able to realize themselves.

The following is a clear example. Certainly many people wish to experience for themselves something of their life before birth. But such aspirations remain futile and pointless if spiritual scientific study has not given them insight into the most subtle and intimate details of the essential nature of what is eternal. If they have really achieved such insight and now want to proceed further in their understanding, then their aspiration, refined and purified, will help them to do so.

7. It is no good saying, "I really want to know about my past life and—for this—I will even study and practice!" Rather, we must be ready to give up all such desires and must renounce them completely. We must learn to learn without ulterior motive. We must be able to rejoice in and be devoted to what we learn for its own sake. Only in this way can we have an aspiration that brings about its realization.

· · ·

8. Whenever I am angry or irritated, I build a wall around me in the soul world and the forces that should develop the eyes of my soul cannot approach me. If, for

example, someone annoys me, he or she sends a soul current into the soul world. But I cannot see this current as long as I am still capable of anger. My anger hides it from me. This is not to say that if I master my anger, I will immediately perceive such soul (or astral) phenomena. For that, I must first develop an inner eye for my soul.

Each of us possesses such an eye in rudimentary form, but it remains ineffective so long as we are still capable of anger. Not that it appears as soon as we have begun to combat the anger in ourselves. Rather, we must continue on, struggling patiently with our anger, until one day we notice that this inner eye in the soul has opened.

Anger is not the only obstacle to the perception of astral phenomena that we must struggle against. Many people become impatient or skeptical if, after having struggled for years to overcome certain traits, clairvoyant seeing still does not manifest. Such people have simply cultivated some qualities while allowing others to grow all the more unhindered. The gift of seeing arises only when we have suppressed *all* the traits hindering the emergence of the latent faculties corresponding to them. Admittedly, the beginnings of clairvoyance (or clairaudience) may appear earlier. But then they are like tender young shoots, vulnerable to all possible errors, and can easily die away if not carefully cultivated and tended.

9. In addition to anger and irritation, we must also struggle against other traits, such as fearfulness, superstition, prejudice, vanity, ambition, curiosity, the urge to gossip, and the tendency to discriminate on the basis of such outer characteristics as social status, gender, race,

and so on. We may have difficulty in understanding that the struggle against such traits has anything to do with increasing our cognitive abilities. Yet every occultist knows that much more depends on these things than on our ability to expand our intelligence and practice artificial exercises. Misunderstandings can easily arise if, for example, we believe that the injunction to overcome fear means becoming foolhardy; or that to fight against discrimination based on social status or race means becoming blind to the differences among people. The fact is that we learn to recognize these differences for what they are only when we are no longer caught up in prejudice. Even in ordinary life, fear of a thing prevents us from seeing it properly. In this sense, racial prejudice prevents us from seeing into a human soul. The esoteric student must take such ordinary common sense and perfect it inwardly with great sensitivity and precision.

10. We place an obstacle in the path of our esoteric development whenever we say something without first having carefully refined and purified it in our thoughts. This can best be made clear by an example: If someone says something to me that I must respond to, I must make an effort to pay more attention to the other person's beliefs, feelings, and even prejudices than to anything I myself might add to the conversation at that moment. In other words, if one is on an occult path one must dedicate oneself conscientiously to schooling an impeccable sense of tact or delicacy. We must learn to gauge the significance for another person of having his or her opinion contradicted by ours. This does not mean that we should hold

back our opinions. There is no question of that. But we should listen to the other person as carefully as possible and formulate our response on the basis of what we have heard. Once again it is a question of a single thought arising in us when we are in such situations. We know that we are on the right path when this thought lives within us so strongly that it becomes part of our character. This thought is: "It does not matter if what I think differs from what the other person thinks. What matters is that, as a result of what I can contribute to the conversation, the other discovers what is right out of themselves." Permeating ourselves with thoughts of this kind seals our character and conduct with the mark of gentleness. Such gentleness is one of the main methods of esoteric schooling. Gentleness removes obstacles, opening our soul and spirit organs. But harshness—callousness—frightens away the soul forms that should awaken the eyes of the soul.

11. As we develop gentleness, another trait begins to form in our souls: quiet attention to all the subtleties of soul life surrounding us, together with the utter stillness of our own soul's activity. If we achieve this, then what is taking place in the soul life around us helps our own soul unfold and grow organically, just as sunlight helps plants to flourish. Thus, patient gentleness and stillness open the soul to the world of souls and our spirit to the country of spirits.

"Abide in calm single-mindedness and solitude. Close your senses to all that they brought you before you entered on the path of esoteric training. Bring all the thoughts that habitually ebbed and flowed within you to rest. Become perfectly still and inwardly silent. And wait patiently for the higher worlds to fashion the eyes and ears of your soul.

"Do not expect to see and hear in the worlds of soul and spirit right away. For what you are doing now is merely a contribution to the training of your higher senses. Not until you have these senses will you be able to see with the eyes of the soul and hear with the ears of the spirit. Once you have been established for a while in calm and solitude, then go about your ordinary daily work. Have this thought deeply imprinted within you: *One day when I am ready for it I shall receive what I am to receive.* Therefore do not be tempted to attract to yourself anything of the higher powers through sheer self-will."

Such are the instructions that every esoteric student receives from his or her teacher at the beginning of the path. If we follow these instructions, we shall perfect ourselves. If we do not follow them, then all our efforts will be in vain. They are not hard to follow if we have patience and constancy. There are no other obstacles than those that we ourselves put in our way, and we can avoid these if we really want to. This must be emphasized repeatedly because many people have a quite false idea of the difficulties of the esoteric path. It is in a certain sense easier to take the first steps on this path than it is to cope with the most mundane problems of daily life without the help of esoteric training.

Only such information is communicated in this book as poses no kind of danger to the health of body or soul. There are, of course, other approaches that lead more quickly to the same goal. But such faster ways have nothing to do with the path presented here because they have certain human consequences that are considered undesirable to anyone experienced in esoteric practices. Since bits of information about these other ways are at times made public, an explicit warning must be sounded against them. For reasons known only to an initiate, such practices can never be described openly and in their true form. The fragments that appear here and there cannot lead to anything positive, but will only undermine health, happiness, and peace of mind. If we do not wish to entrust ourselves to dark powers, whose true nature and origin we do not know, we shall do well to leave such other approaches alone.

12. At this point, something may be said concerning the environment in which the exercises of our esoteric training should be practiced. This has a certain importance, yet it must be understood that the requirements vary from person to person. Someone practicing esoterically in an environment entirely pervaded by selfish interests—such as is found in the modern struggle for survival—should be aware that such interests affect the development of one's soul organs. The inner laws of these organs are, of course, strong enough to prevent such influences from causing real harm. A lily cannot turn into a thistle, no matter how inappropriate its surroundings; nor can the eyes of the soul develop into something other than what they were intended to be, even when they are worked upon by the self-seeking interests of our modern cities. Nevertheless, whatever our circumstances, it is good to practice the

exercises whenever possible in the quiet peacefulness, inner dignity, and charm of nature.

The ideal situation would be to pursue our esoteric training among green plants and sunny mountains, surrounded by the loveliness of nature's simplicity. This would produce a harmony in our inner organs that would never be possible in modern cities. In other words, a person who has grown up surrounded by fragrant pines, snowy peaks, and the quiet bustle of forest animals and insects is better prepared for esoteric work than the person born in the city. Yet none of us, even if we must live in a city, should fail to nourish the organs developing in their soul and spirit with the inspired teachings of spiritual science. If we cannot see the forests turning green day by day each spring, we should at least nourish our hearts with the lofty teachings of the Bhagavad Gita, the Gospel of St. John, and Thomas à Kempis, and with the findings of spiritual science.

Many paths lead to the summit of insight; but it is essential to chose the right one. A person well versed in esoteric practices can say much about these paths that may seem peculiar to the uninitiated. For example, we may have advanced quite far along the esoteric way; we may be standing, as it were, on the threshold, where soul eyes and spirit ears open. Then we are lucky enough to take a trip across the ocean. Seeing the sea calm or stormy, as the case may be, the scales fall from the eyes of the soul—and suddenly we are able to see, we become seers. Another student, at a similar point in his or her development, may be hit by a hard stroke of fate that would paralyze the strength and undermined the energy of any ordinary person. Because the student is on the esoteric path, it becomes the opportunity for illumination. Again, we may persevere patiently, for years, without noticeable results. Then suddenly, as we sit in silent meditation in our room, we find ourselves surrounded by a spiritual light. The walls disappear and become transparent to the soul. A new world spreads out before our eyes which now see, sounding forth for the ears of our spirit, which now hear.

CHAPTER 5

REQUIREMENTS
FOR ESOTERIC TRAINING

1. The requirements or conditions for entering into esoteric training were not arbitrarily devised by any human
being. They arise naturally out of the nature of esoteric
knowledge itself. Just as we cannot become painters if we
are unwilling to handle a paintbrush, so we cannot receive esoteric training if we refuse to meet the conditions
an esoteric teacher considers necessary. Strictly speak-
ing, such teachers can give us only guidance. Whatever
they say should be taken in this spirit. They have passed
through the stages that prepare one for cognition of the
higher worlds. They know from experience what is
needed. But it depends entirely upon our own free will
whether or not we choose to walk the same path as they
followed. Were we to ask an esoteric teacher to allow us
to enter esoteric training, but were unwilling to meet the
conditions, it would be like saying to a painting teacher,
"Teach me to paint, but please excuse me from having to
touch a brush."

A spiritual teacher has nothing to offer a student who does not, of his or her own free will, first come to meet the teacher. Yet it is not enough simply to have a vague wish for higher knowledge. Many people have this wish. But this wish alone, without the willingness to meet the specific requirements of esoteric training, achieves nothing. All those who complain that following the path is not easy should remember this. If we cannot, or do not want to, meet such demanding conditions, we should simply give up the training for the time being. Certainly, these conditions are strict, yet they are not harsh, and carrying them out not only should be, but must be, a free deed.

2. Without this fact of our own free choice, the requirements imposed by a spiritual teacher might easily seem coercive to our soul or conscience. Esoteric training has to do with the education of our inner life, and the spiritual teacher counsels us to this end. Nothing that flows from our own free decision can be called coercion. Were we to ask a teacher, "Tell me your secrets, but leave my ordinary, habitual perceptions, feelings, and ideas untouched," we would be asking the impossible. With this attitude, we would be seeking to satisfy only our curiosity, our desire for information—and we would never attain esoteric wisdom.

3. What follows is a description of the series of conditions to be met by the student. It should be noted that none of these requires complete perfection; we need only strive toward that goal. No one can fulfill these conditions completely, but everyone can set out on the path to their

fulfillment. It is our attitude and our will to begin that are important.

4. The first requirement is that we turn our attention to the improvement of our physical and mental or spiritual health. Our health does not in the first place depend on us. Yet we can make an effort to improve it. Sound understanding—healthy cognition—occurs only in a healthy human being. Esoteric schooling does not exclude unhealthy people, but demands that they have the will to lead a healthy life. Such health depends upon achieving the greatest possible independence and autonomy. As a rule, the good advice that others give us, whether we want it or not, is quite unnecessary. We should strive to take care of ourselves.

With regard to physical health, warding off harmful influences is more important than anything else. To fulfill our obligations, we often have to do things that are not conducive to our health. Indeed, in certain cases we must learn to place responsibility above health. Yet there is much that we can give up, if only we have the good will to do so! Certainly, duty is often more important than health and sometimes even than life itself. Gratification, however, should never be the first priority. For the student of the esoteric way, pleasure should be only a means to health and life. Here we must be completely honest and truthful with ourselves. It is no use leading an ascetic life, if this arises out of the same motives of gratification as do other pleasures. Some people gain the same satisfaction from asceticism that others gain from tippling, and we cannot expect this kind of asceticism to be useful for higher knowledge.

Many people blame everything that seems to hinder their spiritual progress on their outer circumstances. They claim that they cannot work on themselves in their present life situations. It may indeed be desirable to change our situation for other reasons, but we do not need to do so for our esoteric training. All we need to do for this is promote our bodily and mental health as much as we can, given our present circumstances. Whatever we do, even the smallest task, can benefit the whole of humanity. It is a much greater act of soul to be clear about how necessary every small and even menial task is to the whole than to think: "This work is too low for me. I am called to something higher."

Therefore it is especially important for a student to strive for complete mental and spiritual health. An unhealthy inner life impedes our access to higher knowledge. Clear, calm thinking, and reliable sensations and feelings are essential. Nothing should be further from us than any tendency toward fantasy, excitability, nervousness, inflation, and fanaticism. We must acquire a sound eye for all that life presents to us. We must learn to cope confidently with life. We must learn to allow things to speak to us quietly, letting them work upon us. We must make every effort to meet life's demands wherever and whenever necessary. We should avoid all exaggeration and one-sidedness in our judgments and feelings. If we cannot meet these conditions, we will not experience the higher worlds, but only the world of our own imagination; instead of following the truth, we will be guided by our own opinions. It is better to be "down to earth" than inflated and full of fantasies.

5. The second requirement is that we feel ourselves to be a part of the whole of life. Much is involved in fulfilling this condition. But each can approach it in our own way. For instance, if I am a schoolteacher and a pupil does not live up to my wishes, I should direct my feeling not at the pupil but first at myself. I should feel myself so at one with my pupil that I can ask, "Is this pupil's shortcoming not perhaps my own fault?" Instead of blaming the pupil, I should rather reflect upon how I might change my own behavior and so help the pupil meet my expectations in the future.

This kind of attitude will gradually change our whole way of thinking—about the greatest as well as the least of things. For example, I will look upon criminals differently. I will now withhold my judgment and contemplate our common humanity, thinking: "I am a human being just as this person is. Perhaps it was only my upbringing, which my situation in life has given me, that spared me this fate." Then I will reflect that criminals, who are my brothers and sisters in humanity, might have turned out very differently had they received the attention and encouragement my mentors gave me. I will be led to reflect that I have received something that was withheld from them—that my good fortune comes at their expense.

It is then but a small step to the insight that, as a member or organ of humanity as a whole, I am jointly responsible, with all human beings, for everything that happens. This insight should not, of course, be immediately translated into political agitation in the world. It should be calmly cultivated in the soul. By this means it

change is a matter of cultivating a good soul attitude + then letting it manifest in our actions

will gradually come to expression in my outer actions. Indeed, in such matters, we can begin only by reforming ourselves. To make general demands for social and political reform on the basis of such insights is fruitless. It is easy to say how other people should be, but students of esoteric knowledge must work in the depths and not on the surface. It would therefore be quite wrong to connect the demands of esoteric schooling with any external demand for reform or even political change. The education of the spirit has nothing to do with such things. Political activists generally know what to ask of other people, but they hardly ever talk about asking anything of themselves.

6. The third requirement of esoteric training is intimately connected to the second. It requires that we win through to the conviction that thoughts and feelings are as important for the world as actions. We should recognize that when we hate our fellow human beings it is just as destructive as when we physically strike them. This brings us once more to the insight that anything we do for our own improvement benefits not just ourselves but also the world. The world benefits as much from pure feelings and thoughts as from good deeds. Indeed, as long as we do not believe in the world significance of our inner lives, we are not ready to take up esoteric training. And we only rightly believe in the meaning of our inner lives, our souls, when we care for our souls and perform our inner work as if it were at least as real as our outer work. We must know that what we feel has as much impact upon the world as the work done by our hands.

7. With this, the fourth requirement is already stated. We must acquire the conviction that our true nature does not lie without but within. We can achieve nothing spiritually if we regard ourselves merely as a product, a result, of the physical world. The very basis of esoteric training is feeling that we are soul-spiritual beings. Once we have made this feeling our own, we are ready to distinguish between our inner sense of duty and outer success. We learn to recognize that there is no necessary and immediate correlation between these. As esoteric students, we must find the middle ground between following the demands of the world and doing what we see as the right thing to do. We must not force upon others something that they cannot understand, but at the same time we must be free of the urge to do only what those around us recognize and approve of. Only the inner voice of the soul, as it honestly strives for higher knowledge, can confirm our truths. Yet we must also learn as much as possible about our environment and find out what is useful and good for it. And, if we do so, we will develop within ourselves what esoteric science calls "the spiritual scales" or the "balance"—on one of whose trays lies a helpful heart, open to the needs of the world, and on the other, inner firmness and unshakable endurance.

8. This brings us to the fifth requirement: steadfastness in following through on a resolution once it has been made. Nothing should lead us to abandon something we have decided upon except the insight that we have made a mistake. Each resolution we make is a force that works in its own way—even when it is not immediately successful

in the area where it is first applied. Success is crucial only when we act out of longing. But any action motivated by craving is worthless from the point of view of the higher world. In the higher world, love is the only motivation for action. As esoteric students, all that stirs us to action must be subsumed in love. If we act out of love we shall never tire of transforming our resolutions into deeds, no matter how often we may have failed in the past.

As a result, we do not judge a deed on the basis of its *outer* effect on other people but take satisfaction in the act itself of carrying out our actions. We must learn to offer up our deeds, our very essence, to the world—regardless of how our offering may be received. To be esoteric students, we must be prepared for this life of sacrifice and service.

9. The sixth requirement is that we develop the feeling of gratitude for all that we receive. We should know that our very existence is a gift from the whole universe. How much is necessary for human beings to receive and sustain their existence! We owe so much to nature and to other people. Grateful thoughts such as these must become second nature for those engaged in esoteric training. If we do not give ourselves fully to such thoughts, we shall never develop the *all-embracing love* we need to attain higher knowledge. Only if I love something can it reveal itself to me. And every revelation should fill me with thankfulness, for I am made richer by it.

10. All the above conditions come together in the seventh: always to understand life as these conditions demand. In so doing, we create the possibility of giving our

lives the stamp of unity. All the different expressions of our life will then be in harmony and not contradict each other. And this will prepare us for the calm, inner peace we must develop during the first steps in esoteric training.

11. If we are sincerely and genuinely willing to meet these requirements, then we are in a position to commit ourselves to esoteric training. We are then ready to follow the advice given in this book. Some people may find many of these suggestions too outward, too related to external life. Perhaps they did not expect the course of esoteric training to unfold in such strict forms. But everything in our inner life must develop through something outward. Just as a painting that is still only in the painter's head cannot be said really to exist, so esoteric training cannot be said to exist if there is no outward expression of it. Once we know that the outer must express the inner, we can no longer hold the strict forms in low regard. It is true that the spirit is more important than the form—which indeed is nothing at all without the spirit—but the spirit would remain idle if it did not create a form for itself.

12. These requirements are intended to make us strong enough to fulfill the further demands that spiritual training inevitably imposes. If we lack the proper foundation that meeting these conditions provides, we will face each new challenge with misgivings. We will not have the belief in people necessary for esoteric work. To believe in and love humanity is the basis of all striving for the truth. Our striving must be built upon trust and love for humanity—although it does not begin there. Rather, it must flow

out of the soul's own forces. And this love for humanity must gradually expand into love for all beings, and indeed for all existence.

If we are successful in this, we shall have a deep love for all that is constructive and creative. Our natural inclination will be to avoid all destructiveness. As esoteric students, we must never destroy for the sake of destroying— neither in deeds nor in thoughts, words, or feelings. Growth and development must be our joy. We should lend our hand to destruction only if we are able to bring new life out of what we destroy. This does not mean that we should stand idly by while wickedness prevails. On the contrary, in every evil we must seek out the elements that allow us to transform it into good. We will then see more and more clearly that the best way to combat wickedness and imperfection is to create what is good and whole. We cannot create something out of nothing, but we can transform what is incomplete into something more perfect. The more we strengthen our creative tendencies, the sooner we will find ourselves capable of the right attitude toward whatever is bad and imperfect.

13. Anyone who enters esoteric training must realize that its purpose is to build up, not tear down. Therefore we should bring to it a desire to work sincerely and devotedly, not to criticize and destroy. We should become capable of reverence, because we are to learn things we do not yet know. We should look reverently toward what opens before us. Work and reverence are the fundamental attitudes expected of us as esoteric students. When we experience a lack of progress in our training, despite what

we consider our unceasing effort, it is because we have not fully and properly understood the meaning of work and reverence. Work undertaken for the sake of results is the least likely to produce them, and learning unaccompanied by reverence is unlikely to advance us far. Love for the work, not for the results, alone moves us forward. And if we strive for healthy thinking and sound judgment, we will not blunt our reverence with doubt and distrust.

14. Simply listening to what others say with reverence and devotion, rather than immediately opposing it with our own opinions, need not lead to our becoming slavishly dependent upon them. Those who have achieved something on the path to knowledge know that they owe everything to patient listening and assimilation, not to their own obstinate personal opinions. We must always remember that where we have already formed a conclusion we cannot learn anything. If we desire only to judge, therefore, we can learn nothing. Esoteric training, however, depends on learning. As esoteric students, our willingness to learn should be unconditional. It is far better to withhold our judgment on something we do not understand than to condemn it. We can leave understanding until later.

The more levels of cognition we attain, the more we need to be able to listen attentively, calmly, and reverently. For the work of cognizing the truth—indeed, all activity and life in the world of the spirit—is infinitely more subtle and delicate than what we do in the course of our ordinary life and thinking in the physical world. The further our horizon expands, the subtler the work we must perform. That is why there are so many differing "views" and "perspectives" concerning the higher realms. In reality, of course, there is only *one* view of higher truths. We can reach this view if, by work and reverence, we have risen to the stage of actually beholding the truth. Only if we are insufficiently prepared, and form opinions on the basis of our favorite ideas and habitual thoughts, will our view differ from the only true one. Just as there cannot be different opinions regarding a mathematical theorem, so there cannot be different views about things in the higher worlds. But, in order to arrive at such a "view," we must prepare ourselves. If we bear this in mind, we will not be surprised by the conditions required by a spiritual teacher.

Certainly, truth and the higher life dwell within the human soul where each one of us can, and must, find them. But they lie deep within, and can only be brought up from the depths after the obstacles have been cleared away. Only a person experienced in esoteric science can advise us on how this is to be done. Spiritual science offers this advice. But it does not force truths on anyone and does not proclaim any dogma. It shows a way. Each of us could find his or her way on their own, but perhaps only after reincarnating many times. Esoteric methods shorten the path. They allow us to reach the point where we can collaborate in the worlds where spiritual work advances the human evolution and salvation.

15. This concludes all that may be said for the moment about the attainment of experiences of higher worlds. The next chapter will continue these observations by showing what happens in the supersensible members of our being

(in the soul organism or astral body and in the spirit or thought body) during higher development. Thereby what we have said so far will be seen in a new light and explored more thoroughly.

CHAPTER 6

SOME EFFECTS
OF INITIATION

1. One of the basic principles of true esoteric science is that those who dedicate themselves to it must do so in full consciousness. As students, we should undertake nothing, nor engage in any exercises, whose effects we do not understand. An esoteric teacher, when giving advice or instruction, will always explain what the effects of following the instruction will be on the body, soul, or spirit of the person striving for higher knowledge.

2. The present chapter will describe some of the effects of inner work upon the soul of the esoteric student. Not until we are aware of these effects can we practice the exercises that lead to knowledge of the supersensible worlds in full consciousness. Indeed, only the presence of such full consciousness allows us to be called true students of this path. Authentic spiritual training forbids any groping in the dark. Those who do not wish to carry out their training with open eyes may become mediums, but they will never become seers or clairvoyants as esoteric science uses these terms.

3. Those who practice the exercises described in the previous chapters will first of all experience certain changes in their so-called "soul organism." Only a seer can perceive this organism, which may be compared to a more or less soul-spiritually luminous cloud, whose center is the physical body.[1] All our instincts, desires, passions, ideas, and so on are spiritually visible within this "cloud." For example, sensual desires are perceived in the form of dark red rays radiating in a certain form, while pure and noble thoughts express themselves in radiating red-purple hues. Sharply defined concepts, such as grasped by a logical thinker, are felt as yellowish forms with quite distinct outlines, but the muddled thoughts of confused minds appear indistinct. Intolerant and opinionated thoughts appear sharp, fixed, and inflexible, while thoughts open to the concerns of others appear flexible and changing; and so on.[2]

4. The further we advance in soul development, the more regularly structured our soul organism becomes. This organism remains confused and unstructured in a person whose soul life is still undeveloped. Yet even in such

1. A detailed description of this can be found in my book *Theosophy: An Introduction to the Spiritual Processes at Work in Human Life and in the Cosmos* (Hudson, NY: Anthroposophic Press, 1994).

2. It is important to keep in mind that in all such descriptions "seeing" a color refers to *spiritual seeing* (vision). In terms of clairvoyant cognition "seeing red" means that we have an experience in the soul-spiritual realm that is like the physical experience we have when looking at the color red. Thus, in the case of clairvoyant cognition it is natural to use the expression "seeing red," and that is the only reason why the expression is used. We must keep this in mind to avoid mistaking a color vision for a truly clairvoyant experience.

an unstructured soul organism a clairvoyant can still see a form that stands out clearly from its surroundings. The form extends from the inside of the head to the middle of the physical body. To the clairvoyant it looks like an independent body, containing certain organs. These organs—which we shall now consider—may be seen spiritually in the following areas of the physical body: the first, between the eyes; the second, near the larynx; the third, in the region of the heart; the fourth, in the neighborhood of the pit of the stomach or solar plexus; and the fifth and the sixth, in the lower abdomen or reproductive region.

Because they resemble wheels or flowers, esotericists call these formations *chakras* (wheels) or "lotus flowers." But these expressions are no more accurate than calling the parts of a building "wings." In both cases, we are dealing only with figures of speech, with analogies. In a person whose soul life is undeveloped, the "lotus flowers" are of a darkish color, quiet and unmoving. In a seer, on the other hand, they are in motion, shining forth in different colors. With some differences, the same occurs in the case of mediums—but this does not concern us here.

One of the first things to occur when an esoteric student begins practicing the exercises is that the light of the lotus flowers intensifies; later the flowers will also begin to rotate. When this happens, it means that a person is beginning to have the ability to see clairvoyantly.[3] These

---

3. What was explained in the preceding note regarding the perception of "colors" applies also to these perceptions of "rotation" and indeed of the lotus flowers themselves.

"flowers" are the sense organs of the soul. Their rotation indicates that we are able to perceive the supersensible realm. Until we have developed the astral senses in this way, we cannot see anything supersensible.

5. The spiritual sense organ, which is situated near the larynx, enables us to see clairvoyantly into the way of thinking of other soul beings. It also allows us a deeper insight into the true laws of natural phenomena, while the organ located in the region of the heart opens clairvoyant cognition into the mentality and character of other souls. Whoever has developed this organ is also able to cognize certain deeper forces in plants and animals. With the sense organ situated near the solar plexus, we gain insight into the abilities and talents of other souls and see what role animals, plants, minerals, metals, atmospheric phenomena, and so on play in the household of nature.

6. The organ in the vicinity of the larynx has sixteen "petals" or "spokes"; the one near the heart, twelve; and the one near the solar plexus, ten.

7. Specific soul activities are connected with the development of these sense organs. Whoever practices these activities in a particular way contributes to the development of the corresponding spiritual sense organ. For example, eight of the sixteen petals of the "sixteen-petalled lotus flower" near the larynx were formed in the distant past, in an earlier evolutionary stage. We ourselves contributed nothing to their development. We received these first eight petals as a gift of nature at a time when human consciousness was still dreamlike and dull. These eight petals were already active then, and their activities corresponded to

this state of dim consciousness. As consciousness intensified, these lotus petals then lost their light and ceased their
activity. We ourselves can form the remaining eight petals
through the conscious practice of exercises. This will
make the whole lotus flower shining and mobile.

The acquisition of specific faculties depends upon the
development of each of these sixteen lotus petals. As already implied, however, we can develop only eight of
these petals consciously. The other eight then appear of
their own accord.

8. To develop the *sixteen-petalled lotus flower* we proceed as follows. We direct our care and attention to *eight
specific soul processes* that we usually perform without
care or attention.

The first soul process concerns the way in which we acquire ideas or mental images. As a rule, we leave this to
chance. We happen to see or hear something, and then we
form our concepts on that basis. As long as we behave in
this way, the sixteen-petalled lotus flower remains quite
inactive. But when we begin to discipline ourselves, it begins to move. Discipline here means that we pay attention
to our ideas or mental representations. Each one must become meaningful to us. We must begin to see in every image or idea a specific message about something in the outer
world. Ideas that do not have a meaning for the outer world
should no longer satisfy us. We must guide our conceptual
life to become a true mirror of the outer world. All our
striving must be to eliminate false ideas from the soul.

The second soul process to be considered—much in the
same way as the first—is how we make decisions. Any

decision, even the most trivial, should be made only after thorough, well-reasoned deliberation. We should remove all thoughtless activity and meaningless action from our souls. We must have well-thought-out reasons for all we do. Anything we cannot find a reason for, we must refrain from doing.

The third soul process concerns speech. When we are esoteric students, every word should have substance and meaning. Talk for talking's sake diverts us from the path. We must avoid the ordinary kind of conversation where everyone talks at the same time and topics are indiscriminately jumbled together. This does not mean that we should cut ourselves off from interaction with our fellow human beings. On the contrary, it is precisely in interaction with others that we should learn to make our words meaningful. We should be ready to speak to and answer everyone, but only after having taken thought and thoroughly considered the issue at hand. We should never speak without good reason. We should talk neither too much nor too little.

The fourth soul process concerns the ordering of our outer actions. As esoteric students, we should try to manage our affairs so that they fit both with the affairs of others and with events around us. We should abstain from any behavior that would disturb others or otherwise go against what is happening around us. We should strive to direct our activity so that it integrates harmoniously into our surroundings, our situation in life, and so forth. When a situation prompts us to act, we should consider carefully how best to respond to this prompting. And when we act on our own initiative, we should weigh the consequences of what we intend to do as clearly as we can.

At this point, *the fifth soul process* comes under consideration, namely, the arrangement and organization of our life as a whole. As esoteric students, we must strive to live in harmony with both nature and spirit. We must be neither overhasty, nor slow and lazy. Hyperactivity and laxity should be equally alien to us. We should see life itself as a way of working and arrange it accordingly. We should take care of our health and regulate our habits so that a harmonious life ensues as a consequence.

The sixth soul process has to do with human striving or effort. As esoteric students we must assess our talents and abilities and then act in accordance with this self-knowledge. We should not try to do anything that lies beyond our powers, yet we must always do everything that lies within our powers to do. At the same time, we must set ourselves aspirations connected to humanity's great ideals and obligations. We should not thoughtlessly place ourselves as mere cogs in the vast human machine, but try to understand our tasks and learn to look beyond our daily routines. Hence we should always strive to perfect the performance of our duties.

The seventh soul process involves the effort to learn as much as possible from life. As esoteric students, nothing comes to us in life that does not provide an opportunity to gather experiences useful for the future. Mistakes and imperfections become an incentive to perform more correctly and perfectly whenever a similar situation next arises. In the same way, we can learn from watching others. We should try to gather as rich a treasure of experience as possible, conscientiously drawing on it for advice at all times. We should do nothing without looking back upon the experiences that can help us to decide and act.

Finally, *the eighth soul process*: as esoteric students, we should periodically turn and look inward. We must sink absorbed into ourselves, gently taking counsel with ourselves, shaping and testing our basic principles of life, mentally reviewing what we know, weighing our obligations, pondering the meaning and purpose of life, and so forth. All this has been discussed in earlier chapters and is summarized here only for its connection with the sixteen-petalled lotus flower. The practice of these activities perfects our lotus flower, for the development of clairvoyance depends on such exercises. For example, the more our thoughts and words harmonize with events in the outer world, the more quickly we develop this gift. In contrast, when we think or say something untrue, we destroy something in the bud of the sixteen-petalled lotus flower. In this regard, truthfulness, sincerity, and honesty are constructive forces, while lying, falsity, and insincerity are destructive ones.

On the esoteric path, we must be aware that what matters is not "good intentions," but what we actually do. If I think or say something that does not correspond to reality, I destroy something in my spiritual sense organ, regardless of how good I think my intentions are. Similarly, a child gets burnt when it puts its hands into the fire, even though it acts out of ignorance.

In sum, if we orient these soul processes in the ways outlined here, the sixteen-petalled lotus flower will shine forth in glorious colors and move in accordance with its inherent laws.

It must be noted, however, that the faculty of "seeing" will appear only after a certain level of soul development has been attained. So long as it is still an effort to orient our life in this direction, the gift of seeing will not reveal itself. We are not ready for it if we still need to pay special attention to the activities described here. When living in this way has become second nature to us, then the first signs of seeing or clairvoyance will appear. At that point, we will no longer need to struggle and spur ourselves on to this new way of life; we will live it naturally and effortlessly.

There are certain other, and easier, methods for developing the sixteen-petalled lotus flower. True spiritual science rejects such methods because they lead to the destruction of our physical health and to moral corruption. The instructions presented here may require more time and effort, but they will lead us safely to our goal and can only strengthen our moral life.

9. Certain forms of clairvoyant seeing appear as the result of distortions in the development of the lotus flower. In this case, the seeing is marked not only by illusions and fantastic ideas but also by deviance and instability in daily life. As a result of such warped development, a person may become fearful, jealous, conceited, arrogant, willful, and so on—even though he or she did not have these traits before.

As stated above, eight of the sixteen petals of the lotus flower were developed in the far-distant past and reappear of their own accord during esoteric schooling. The care and attention of the student, therefore, must be directed toward developing the eight new petals. In false approaches to esoteric schooling, the already developed earlier petals can easily appear alone, while the new petals still needing to be formed remain stunted. This happens particularly when not enough attention is paid to logical, level-headed thinking in the training. Of prime importance is that the student of esotericism be a sensible person, devoted to clear thinking. Equally important is to strive for the greatest clarity in speech. When we begin to have a first inkling of the supersensible, we are tempted to talk about it. But this only impedes our development. Until we have gained a certain degree of clarity in these matters, the less we say about them, the better.

At the beginning of our training, we may be surprised to find how little "curiosity" spiritually schooled persons show for our experiences. Indeed, it would be healthiest for us if we said nothing at all about our experiences and instead spoke only about how well or how badly we managed to carry out the exercises or follow our instructions. Those who are schooled spiritually have sources other than a student's own direct account for evaluating his or her progress. Besides, talking about our experiences always somewhat hardens the eight petals we are developing—and these should remain soft and pliable.

An example taken, for the sake of clarity, from ordinary rather than supersensible life will illustrate this point. Suppose I receive news about something and immediately form a judgment about it. Shortly thereafter, I learn more, but the new information does not agree with the first news I received. Hence I am obliged to revise my opinion. The consequence of this, however, is an adverse effect on my sixteen-petalled lotus flower. Had I been more restrained in my judgment and kept quiet about the matter in thought and word until I had reliable grounds to form a judgment, things would have turned out quite differently. Such tact, precision, and delicacy in forming and expressing judgments must gradually become our signature as esoteric students. At the same time, our sensitivity to impressions and experiences will increase. We should let these pass silently through us to create as many reference points as possible when it comes to forming a judgment. If we proceed cautiously in this way, then blue-red and rose-red nuances arise in the lotus petals; if we do not, then dark red and orange nuances appear.

The twelve-petalled lotus flower, near the heart, is formed in a way similar to the sixteen-petalled one.[4] Half of its petals were also already present and active in a past evolutionary stage of humanity. Thus, we do not have to develop those six petals; they appear on their own and begin to rotate when we start working on the other six petals.

---

4. People familiar with the subject matter will recognize in the requirements for the development of the sixteen-petalled lotus flower the instructions Buddha gave his disciples for the "path." However, the point here is not to teach Buddhism but to describe conditions for development that grow out of spiritual science itself. That they agree with certain teachings of Buddha does not make them any less true in themselves.

To promote their development, we must again deliberately orient certain soul activities in a particular direction.

10. We have to realize that the perceptions provided by the various spiritual or soul senses differ in character. The twelve-petalled lotus flower conveys a different perception from the sixteen-petalled one. The sixteen-petalled flower perceives forms. That is, it perceives as a form both another soul's way of thinking and the laws according to which a natural phenomenon unfolds. Such forms are not rigid and unmoving, but mobile and filled with life. A seer who has developed this sense organ can describe—for every way of thinking and natural law—the particular shape in which the thinking or law expresses itself. For example, a vengeful thought has an arrowlike and jagged shape, while a kind thought often has the form of a flower beginning to blossom, and so on. Thoughts that are firm and meaningful are symmetrical and regular; concepts that are unclear have wavy, almost frizzy outlines.

Quite different perceptions come to light through the twelve-petalled lotus flower. These may be roughly characterized in terms of warmth and coldness of soul. Seers, endowed with this sense organ, feel soul warmth or coldness streaming from the figures perceived by the sixteen-petalled lotus flower. This means that a seer who has developed the sixteen-petalled lotus flower, but not the twelve-petalled one, clairvoyantly perceives a kind thought only in terms of its figures described above. If, on the other hand, both organs are developed, then the seer also perceives something—that can be described only as soul warmth—streaming from the thought.

In esoteric schooling one sense organ is never developed apart from the others. The sense organs are always developed together. The above example, therefore, was given only hypothetically, for the sake of clarity.

Developing the twelve-petalled lotus flower gives us profound insight into the processes of nature. Everything growing and maturing radiates soul warmth, while everything undergoing death, destruction, and decay has the quality of soul coldness.

11. *The twelve-petalled lotus flower* is formed in the following way.

First, we pay attention to directing the sequence of our thoughts—this is the so-called "practice of the control of thoughts." Just as thinking true and meaningful thoughts develops the sixteen-petalled lotus flower, so inwardly controlling our thinking processes develops the twelve-petalled flower. Thoughts that flit about like will-o'-the-wisps and follow each other by chance rather than in a logical, meaningful way distort and damage the form of this flower. The more logically our thoughts follow one another and the more we avoid all illogical thinking, the more perfectly this organ develops its proper form.

Therefore whenever we hear an illogical thought, we should immediately allow the correct thought to pass through our mind. But, if we find ourselves in what seems an illogical environment, we should not for that reason unlovingly withdraw in order to further our development. By the same token, we should not feel the immediate urge to correct any illogicality we witness around us. Rather, we should inwardly and very quietly give the thoughts rushing at us from the outside a logical and meaningful direction. We should always strive to maintain this logical direction in our own thinking.

Second, we must bring an equally logical consistency into our actions—this is the practice of the control of actions. Any instability and disharmony in our actions injures the development of the twelve-petalled lotus flower. Therefore, each of our actions should follow logically from whatever action came before. If we act today out of different principles than we did yesterday, we shall never develop the lotus flower in question.

Third, we must cultivate perseverance. As long as we consider a goal we have set ourselves to be right and worthy, we should never let any outside influence deter us from striving to reach it. We should consider obstacles as challenges to be overcome, not as reasons for giving up.

Fourth, we must develop forbearance (or tolerance) toward other people, other beings, and events. We must suppress all unnecessary criticism of imperfection, evil, and wickedness and seek rather to understand everything that comes to meet us. Just as the sun does not withdraw its light from wickedness and evil, so we, too, should not withdraw our understanding and sympathy from anyone. When we meet adversity, we should not indulge in negative judgments but accept the inevitable and try, as best we can, to turn it to the good. Similarly, instead of considering the opinions of others only from our own standpoint, we should try to put ourselves into their position.

Fifth, we must develop openness and impartiality toward all the phenomena of life. This is sometimes called faith or trust. We must learn to approach every person, every being, with trust. Such trust or confidence must inspire all our actions. We should never say, in reply to something said to us, "I don't believe that because it contradicts the opinion I have already formed." Rather, when faced with something new, we must always be willing to test our opinions and views and revise them if necessary. We must always remain receptive to whatever approaches us. We should trust in the effectiveness of whatever we undertake. All doubt and timidity should be banished from our being. If we have a goal, we must have faith in the power of our goal. Even a hundred failures should not be able to take this faith from us. This is the "faith that can move mountains."

Sixth, we must achieve a certain balance in life (or serenity). As esoteric students, we should strive to maintain a mood of inner harmony whether joy or sorrow comes to meet us. We should lose the habit of swinging between being "up one minute and down the next." Instead, we should be as prepared to deal with misfortune and danger as with joy and good fortune.

12. The reader familiar with spiritual scientific literature will recognize in the practice of these six qualities the so-called "six attributes" that a person seeking initiation has to develop. They are mentioned now because of their relationship to the development of the sense organ of the soul called the twelve-petalled lotus flower. Esoteric training may also provide special instructions for bringing this lotus flower to maturity. But here again the fashioning of a regular form for the sense organ depends upon

the development of the qualities or attributes already described. If we ignore the cultivation of these qualities, then this organ will be distorted into a caricature of itself. A certain faculty of seeing may be developed in the process, but as a result of distortion any of the six attributes may be transformed and become bad rather than good. We may become intolerant, fearful, and negative toward our surroundings. For example, we may become sensitive to other people's soul mood and mentality and for this reason avoid or dislike them. This may even go so far that coldness floods our soul whenever we hear opinions contrary to our own with the result that we cannot listen to them or respond belligerently.

13. Were we to add to the practices that have been suggested so far certain other rules which a student can receive only orally from a teacher, then we would be able to accelerate the development of this lotus flower. Nevertheless, the directions already given here definitely lead to true esoteric training. Organizing one's life along these lines is also beneficial for those who cannot or do not wish to undergo esoteric training. These practices will in any case work upon one's soul organism, even if only slowly. For the esoteric student, however, the observation of these fundamental principles is essential.

To attempt an occult training without following these guidelines would be to enter the higher worlds with defective mental eyes. Instead of cognizing the truth, one would be subject only to deceptions and illusions. We might become clairvoyant to a certain extent, but essentially we would be susceptible to an even greater blindness than before. Before beginning esoteric practice we at least stood firmly in the sense world and had a certain foothold in it. Now perhaps we can see behind it, but because we have not gained a firm hold in a higher world, we begin to lose our way there. And this may lead us to lose our ability to distinguish truth and error, and to lose all sense of direction in life.

This is why patience is so necessary in these matters. We must always bear in mind that the instructions of spiritual science may lead us no further than our complete willingness to develop the lotus flowers in a harmonious manner. If these flowers are brought to maturity before they have quietly developed their appropriate forms, then only a distorted travesty of the true form of the flower develops. For while the specific exercises given by spiritual science produce the maturation of the flowers, their form is given by the way of living that has been described.

14. The development of *the ten-petalled lotus flower* near the solar plexus requires cultivating soul care of a particularly subtle and delicate kind. Here it is a matter of learning to consciously control and master the sense impressions themselves. This is especially important in the early stages of clairvoyant seeing. Only by learning to control and master sense impressions can we avoid a source of countless illusions and arbitrary spiritual fantasies.

As a rule we do not realize what controls the occurrence of ideas and memories and how they are called forth. Consider the following: We are riding in a train, wrapped up in our own thoughts, when suddenly our thinking takes a completely new turn—we remember something that happened many years ago. We weave this into our present thoughts. What we do not notice is that our eyes, looking through the window, fell upon a person resembling someone involved in the event we recalled. But we are not conscious of what we saw. We are aware only of the effect it has produced in us. Therefore we think that our memory of the event occurred "of its own accord."

How much in life comes about in this way! Many things we have seen or read play into our lives without our being conscious of the connections. For example, we may dislike a certain color and not know why: we have forgotten that a teacher, who tormented us years ago, used to wear a coat of that color. Countless illusions are based on such connections.

Many things are imprinted into our soul without at the same time being assimilated into our consciousness. For example, we read in the newspaper that a famous person died and we believe—we insist— that we had a "premonition" of this death the day before, even though we saw and heard nothing that could have given rise to the thought. And it is true that, as if spontaneously, the thought that this famous person would die arose in us the day before. A single fact alone escaped our notice. When we visited a friend a few hours before this thought arose, a newspaper lay on the table. We did not read it, but unconsciously our eyes registered the headlines. These announced the critical condition of the celebrity in question. We were unaware of this impression. The effect it produced, however, was our "premonition."

In the light of these examples it is clear that such unconscious relationships present a great source of illusion
and fantasy. The development of the ten-petalled lotus
flower requires that we block off this source. This lotus
flower allows us to perceive deeply hidden soul qualities.
But we can rely on the truth of these perceptions only if
we are completely free of such deceptions. To achieve
this, we must make ourselves masters of what affects us
from the outer world. We must reach the point where we
actually do not receive any impressions that we do not
want. Only a strong inner life can develop this capacity.
It must actually enter our will—and become second nature there—that we allow only those things to work upon
us that we have intentionally focused upon. In other
words, we must be completely unavailable to those impressions to which we have not turned our attention. We
must see only what we want or will to see. What we do
not turn our attention to in fact must not exist for us. The
more lively and energetic our inner soul work becomes,
the more we will achieve this. Students of esoteric training must avoid all mindless gazing and listening. Only
those things that we deliberately focus our eyes and ears
upon must exist for us. We must make it a practice not to
hear what we do not want to hear, no matter what turmoil
is going on around us. Our eyes must become unrecep-
tive to anything we do not choose to focus on. We must
be surrounded as if by a kind of soul armor against all unconscious impressions.

To this end, we turn our care and attention above all to
our thought life.

For example, we must choose a particular thought and then try to think through this thought only thinking such thoughts as we can integrate into it in full consciousness and complete freedom. If any random thoughts arise, we reject them; and if we link one thought with another, we consider carefully how this second thought arose. But this is only the beginning. For instance, if we feel a particular antipathy for something, we combat this feeling and try to develop a conscious relationship to the thing in question. As a result of these kinds of exercises, fewer and fewer unconscious elements interfere with our soul life.

Strict self-discipline of this kind is the only way to develop the true form of the ten-petalled lotus flower. If we wish to pursue this path to higher knowledge and become true esoteric students, our soul life must become a life lived in a state of attention. We must know how to really keep away all that we do not want to pay attention to, or ought not to pay attention to.

If we combine such self-discipline with a practice of meditation consonant with the indications given by spiritual science, the lotus flower located in the solar plexus matures properly. What had only shape and warmth for the spiritual sense organs we have previously described will now contain spiritual light and color. This will reveal to us the gifts and abilities of other souls, as well as the forces and hidden qualities in nature. The color aura of living beings will become visible to us, and everything around us will manifest its soul-like qualities.

It must be admitted that great care and attention to detail are necessary in working on this soul organ because unconscious memories are particularly active here. If this were not so, many people would possess the sense organ in question, since it appears almost immediately upon our ability to control our sense impressions so completely that they are fully under the command of the attention. It is, after all, only the power of the physical senses that keeps this inner soul sense muted, dull, and ineffective.

15. The development of *the six-petalled lotus flower*, located in the center of the body, is more difficult still. Its formation requires that we strive for the complete mastery of our whole being through becoming conscious of our self in such a way that, within this consciousness, body, soul, and spirit are in perfect harmony. Physical activity, the inclinations and passions of the soul, and the thoughts and ideas of the spirit must be brought into perfect accord with each other. We should purify and ennoble the body to such an extent that our physical organs no longer compel us to do anything that is not in the service of our soul and spirit. The body should not urge upon our soul desires and passions that contradict pure and noble thinking. Nor should the spirit rule the soul with compulsory duties and laws like a slave driver. Rather, the soul should follow these obligations and laws of its own free inclination. As students we should not think of duties as something imposed upon us that we grudgingly perform; we should perform them because we love them.

This means that the soul must become free, poised in perfect balance between the senses and the spirit. We must reach the point in our development where we can surrender to our sense nature because it has been so purified that it no longer has the power to drag us down. We should no longer need to restrain our passions because these follow the right course on their own. Indeed, as long as we still need to mortify ourselves, we cannot advance beyond a certain level of esoteric training. Virtues that we have to force upon ourselves are without value.

As long as we still have cravings, these will interfere with our training even when we try not to give in to them. It makes no difference whether the desires arise from the body or the soul. For example, if we abstain from a certain stimulant in order to purify ourselves by denying ourselves the pleasure it affords, this will help us only if the body does not suffer any discomforts in the process. For the discomfort we experience only indicates that the body still *craves* the stimulant—and therefore abstention is useless. In such cases, we may have to renounce our aspirations for the time being and wait for more favorable physical conditions—perhaps in a later life. In certain situations, a sensible renunciation is a much greater accomplishment than the continued striving for something that cannot be achieved under existing conditions. Such sensible renunciation advances our development more than the opposite course of persisting despite indications to the contrary.

16. The development of the six-petalled lotus flower brings us into relation with beings of the higher worlds, but only with those whose existence is also revealed in the soul world. In esoteric training, the development of this lotus flower is recommended only after we have advanced to the point where we can lift our spirit into a still higher world. Entry into the actual spirit world must always go

along with the development of the lotus flowers. Otherwise, confusion and uncertainty follow. We would learn to see, but we would lack the faculty of rightly evaluating what we saw.

Of course, the requirements for the development of the six-petalled lotus flower are in themselves already a kind of guarantee against confusion and instability. For once we have achieved a perfect balance between the senses (body), the passions (soul), and ideas (spirit), we are no longer easily confused. Still, something more than this assurance is needed when, having developed the six-petalled lotus flower, we begin to perceive living and autonomous beings that belong to a world very different from the world of the physical senses. The development of the lotus flowers is not enough to give us confidence and certainty in these worlds. We have to have still higher organs at our disposal.

We shall now discuss the development of these higher organs before continuing the discussion of the other lotus flowers and the further organization of the "soul body."[5]

· · ·

17. The development of the "soul body," just mentioned, enables us to perceive supersensible phenomena.

---

5. Obviously, the term "soul body" in its literal meaning presents a paradox—as does many another term of spiritual science. Nevertheless, we use this expression because the clairvoyant perception in question is experienced spiritually in the same way as the body is in the physical realm.

But if we are to find our way about in this world, we cannot remain at this stage of development. Simply achieving mobility of the lotus flowers is not enough. We must be able to regulate and control—by our own will and in full consciousness—the movements of our spiritual organs. Otherwise, we become a plaything of outer forces and powers. To avoid this, we must be able to hear what is called the "inner word." And for this we need to develop not only the soul body, but also the ether body.

The ether body is the subtle body that is seen by clairvoyants as a kind of double of the physical body. One might say it is an intermediate stage between the physical body and the soul body.[6] If we have the gift of clairvoyant faculties, we can consciously think away the physical body of a person standing before us. This is basically the same as an exercise in attention, except that it occurs on a higher level. Just as we can turn our attention away from things around us, with the result that they no longer exist for us, so those who are clairvoyant can completely erase the physical body from their perception. Consequently, the physical body becomes totally transparent. When clairvoyants erase the physical body of someone standing before them, what still remains before their soul eyes are the so-called ether body and the soul body, which is larger than the physical and ether bodies and permeates both.

The ether body has about the same size and shape as the physical body and so occupies approximately the same space as the physical body. It is an extremely delicate and

---

6. See also its description in my book *Theosophy*.

finely organized structure.[7] Its basic color is one not found among the seven colors of the rainbow. As we become able to observe the ether body, we learn to see a color that actually does not exist for sensory observation. It is best compared to the color of young peach blossoms. Of course, to study the ether body alone , we have to remove the soul body from our perception through an exercise of attentiveness similar to the one mentioned above. If this is not done, the appearance of the ether body will be changed by the soul body, which permeates it completely.

18. The tiny particles of the human ether body are in constant movement. Countless currents stream through it in all directions. These currents maintain and regulate life. Hence every living body has an ether body. Plants and animals have one, and an attentive observer may even see traces of the ether body in minerals. Without esoteric training, these currents and movements are completely independent of our will and consciousness. They are like the activities of the heart or the stomach, which are likewise independent of our will. As long, then, as we do not take our development into our own hands and begin to work on developing supersensible faculties, the ether body maintains its complete independence from us.

Further esoteric development, therefore, consists precisely in adding to those movements of the ether body,

---

7. I have to ask physicists not to be put off by the term "ether body." The word "ether" is intended merely to express the delicacy of the formation under consideration. What is said here need not be connected in any way with the "ether" in certain hypotheses in physics.

which are independent of our consciousness, currents and movements that we ourselves have consciously produced.

19. By the time esoteric training has reached the stage when the lotus flowers begin to rotate (or move), we have already done much of the preparatory work needed to produce certain specific currents and movements in the ether body. The goal of our development is now to form a kind of *central point* near the physical heart from which currents and movements spread in manifold spiritual colors and shapes. In reality, of course, this center is not really a "point," but rather a quite complex formation, a marvelous organ, shining and shimmering spiritually in a great variety of colors and revealing quickly changing shapes of great regularity.

Further forms and streams of color radiate out from this central organ to the other parts of the body and even beyond it, permeating and illuminating the entire soul body. The most important currents, however, flow to the lotus flowers, permeating each petal and regulating their rotation. The currents then flow out from the tips of the petals and disappear into the surrounding space. The more developed a person is, the greater the circumference formed by these spreading currents.

20. The twelve-petalled lotus flower is closely related to the central point described above. All the currents flow directly into and through this "point." Thence, on the one side, some currents continue up to the sixteen- and the two-petalled lotus flowers, while on the other, lower side, they flow down to the eight-, six-, and four-petalled flowers. This arrangement accounts for the fact that, in

esoteric training, especially careful attention is paid to the development of the twelve-petalled lotus flower. If any mistake is made here, the development of the whole system is thrown into disorder.

We can see therefore how very delicate and intimate a matter esoteric training is, and with what precision we must proceed if everything is to develop in the right way. This is why only those who have themselves experienced what they teach can give instructions for the development of supersensible faculties, for only on this basis are they in a position to know whether their instructions are producing the right results.

21. When we follow the instructions given here, we acquire currents and movements in our ether body which are in harmony with the laws and evolution of the world to which we belong. For this reason, instructions in esoteric training always mirror the great laws of world evolution. These instructions consist in the meditation and concentration exercises mentioned in this book, as well as other similar exercises. Applied properly, these exercises produce the effects that have been described.

Students of the spirit should set aside certain times when they completely permeate their souls with the content of such exercises, thereby becoming, as it were, inwardly filled with them. We begin with simple exercises, above all those designed to deepen and spiritualize our powers of reasoning and understanding. Such exercises render our thinking free and independent of all sense impressions and experiences. We concentrate our thinking in one point, so to speak, over which we then have complete control. In the process, a temporary center is created for the currents of the ether body. In other words, initially the central point is not located near the heart, but in the head. Seers can perceive it there as the starting point of the above-mentioned etheric movements.

Only an esoteric training that begins by creating this temporary center in the head can be completely successful. If we were to develop the center near the heart immediately, we would certainly still gain a glimpse into the higher worlds at the early stages of clairvoyance, but we would have no true insight into the connection between these higher worlds and the material world of the senses. It is absolutely essential, however that human beings at the present stage of world evolution understand this connection. As seers, we must not become dreamers: we must always keep both feet firmly on the ground.

22. Once the temporary center in the head has been properly stabilized, further practice of the concentration exercises transfers it downward, into the vicinity of the larynx. The movements and currents of the ether body then spread out from there, illuminating the soul space around us.

23. Further practice of these exercises will enable us to determine the position of the ether body for ourselves. Before entering esoteric training, the position of the ether body depended upon forces coming from outside and from the physical body. But, as we advance successfully in our development, we become able to turn the ether body in all directions, using the currents that flow roughly parallel to the hands and whose center lies in the two-petalled lotus

flower near the eyes. This is possible because the currents flowing from the larynx form rounded shapes, some of which flow toward the two-petalled lotus flower and thence continue on as wave-like currents along the hands.

These currents then ramify and branch out in the most delicate way to form a kind of net. This becomes a sort of membranous network at the boundary of the ether body. Before we began practicing, the ether body was not enclosed. The currents of life flowed in and out from the universal ocean of life directly and unhindered. Now, however, all influences from the outside have to pass through this thin web or skin. As a result, we become sensitive to these outer currents and begin to perceive them.

The time has now come to give this complex system of currents and movements a center near the heart. This is done by continuing the concentration and meditation exercises. At the same time, this moment marks the stage of our development at which we receive the gift of the "inner word." Henceforth, all things have a new sense and meaning for us. They become, as it were, spiritually audible to us in their inmost essence; they speak to us of their true nature. What happens is that the currents described above put us in touch with the inner life of the cosmos to which we belong. We begin to participate in the life around us and let this life reverberate in the movements of our lotus flowers.

24. With this, we enter the world of the spirit. We become able to understand the words of the great teachers of humanity in a new way. The Buddha's sermons or the Gospels, for example, work upon us in a completely new

way. They stream through us, permeating us with a bliss we never imagined before, for the melody of their words harmonizes with the movements and rhythms we have formed within ourselves. Now we can know directly that beings such as the Buddha or the writers of the Gospels do not voice their own revelations but only what flows into them from the innermost essence of things.

Here I may point out something that can be understood only in light of what we have learned about the ether body. Many educated people today find the repetitions in the Buddha's discourses difficult to understand. But once we embark upon the esoteric path we learn to enjoy dwelling on these repetitions with our inner senses. For these repetitions correspond to certain rhythmical movements in the ether body. And when we surrender to the repetitions in perfect inner peace, our inner movements blend harmoniously with them. When we listen to the word-melodies of the Buddha's teaching, our life becomes infused with the secrets of the universe. For the movements of Buddha's word-melodies mirror cosmic rhythms that also consist of repetitions and regular returns to earlier rhythms.

25. Spiritual science speaks of four faculties that must be acquired on the so-called preparatory path, or path of probation, before one can advance to higher knowledge. The first is the ability to distinguish in our thinking between truth and appearance—between what is true and what is simply opinion. The second is the ability to value truth and reality rightly in relation to appearances. The third consists in the application of the six qualities mentioned in the preceding chapter: control of thoughts, control of actions,

perseverance, tolerance, faith, and equanimity. The fourth is the love of inner freedom.

26. Mere intellectual understanding of what is contained in these faculties is quite useless. They must be integrated in the soul and establish inner habits there.

Take, for example, the first faculty of distinguishing between truth and appearance. Here we must train ourselves so that it becomes second nature to discriminate between what is not essential and what is meaningful in everything we encounter. Such training requires us to practice this discrimination with regard to everything we observe in the outer world. We must seek to do this at all times, and with complete inner calm and patience. Eventually, our eyes will come to turn as easily to what is real and true as they turned before to what was not essential. And the truth of Goethe's words that "Everything transient is but a symbol" will become a natural conviction in our souls. The same process also applies, of course, to the development of the other three faculties mentioned above.

27. Under the influence of these faculties, now become inner soul habits, the delicate human ether body becomes transformed. The practice of the first—"distinguishing between truth and appearance"—forms the center for the lotus flower in the head and, at the same time, prepares the center near the larynx. The actual formation of these centers, however, depends upon carrying out the concentration exercises mentioned above. The concentration exercises develop and form the centers, while the practice of the four inner habits of soul brings them to maturity.

Once the center near the larynx is prepared, the second faculty—that of "rightly valuing the true over inessential appearance"—enables us to freely control, cover, and mark the boundaries of the ether body with the web or network. At this point, if we value the truth above all things and make this second nature, we gradually begin to "see" spiritual facts. But we should never make the mistake of thinking that a rational, intellectual evaluation of what is significant should determine our actions. Even the smallest acts and the least chores have a significance in the great household of the cosmos. It is a matter of becoming conscious of this significance, of not undervaluing the everyday affairs of life and of learning to value them rightly.

We have already discussed the six virtues (control of thoughts and actions, perseverance, patience, faith, and equanimity) that combine to form the third faculty. These virtues are connected with the development of the twelve-petalled lotus flower near the heart. It is to this region, as we indicated above, that we must guide the ether body's current of life. The fourth faculty—that of "desiring liberation" (love of inner freedom)—serves to bring the ether organ near the heart to maturity. Once this love of freedom has become a soul habit, we ourselves become free of all that is connected only with capacities of an individual, personal nature. We cease to look at things from our own separate, particular point of view. The boundaries set by the narrow self, which chain us to this perspective, vanish. And the mysteries of the spiritual world may enter our inner life.

This is the sought-for liberation. The fetters of the narrow self force us to view beings and things in a personal way. To attain higher knowledge, we must become free of these fetters of a personal and limited way of looking at things.

28. One can see from all this that the instructions drawn from spiritual science work decisively into the innermost depths of human nature. The directions regarding the four faculties are instructions of this kind. They are to be found in one form or another in all the philosophies that acknowledge the existence of a spiritual world. The founders of such philosophies did not bequeath these instructions to humanity on the basis of some vague feeling. They did so because they were great initiates. They formed their moral precepts on the basis of their cognition. They knew that these precepts would affect humanity's finer and nobler nature, and they wanted their disciples gradually to train this nature. To live by such world views and philosophies means to work on perfecting ourselves spiritually. Only when we do this do we serve the cosmos as a whole. To perfect oneself in this way is by no means selfish. As long as we are imperfect human beings, we are also imperfect servants of humanity and the world. The more perfected we are, the better we can serve the whole. The saying, "If a rose is beautiful, it makes the garden beautiful," is also true of human beings.

29. The founders of the greatest philosophies are therefore great initiates. Their teachings flow into human souls and by this means the whole world advances with humanity. Indeed, they worked consciously for the progress of

human evolution. Thus we can understand the content of their teachings only when we bear in mind that it is drawn from knowledge of the inmost depths of human nature. The initiates were great gnostics, seekers after knowledge—*they knew*—and they shaped humanity's ideals out of their knowledge. We, too, can approach these great leaders of humanity if, in our own development, we seek to raise ourselves to their heights.

30. After the ether body begins to develop in the way described above, a whole new life opens up before us. To find our way in this new life, we need the enlightenment that esoteric training, at the appropriate moment, can provide. For example, at a certain point, the sixteen-petalled lotus flower enables us to see spiritually the beings and forms of a higher world. But now we must learn to distinguish among the forms. They differ depending on whether they were caused by an object or a being. At first, we should pay attention to how our own thoughts and feelings can influence these forms—strongly or only slightly or perhaps not at all. Some forms will change immediately if, when we first see them, we think, "That is beautiful," and then, in the course of contemplation, change that to "That is useful." These forms that characteristically change with our every thought or feeling are those produced by minerals or human-made objects. Forms arising from plants change less easily in response to our thoughts and feelings, and those of animals even less so.

These latter forms are full of life and movement. This mobility is due partly to the influence of our thoughts and feelings and partly to causes over which we have no

control. In the world of forms, however, there are some
that remain, initially at least, outside human influence. By
inner study, we can determine to our satisfaction that such
forms may be ascribed neither to minerals or artificial objects, nor to plants or animals. Further clarity is gained
when we next observe the forms that we know result from
people's emotions, instincts, passions, and so on. We find
that our own thoughts and feelings still have an influence
on these, although it is relatively slight. Thus, after elim-
inating all these, there still remain some forms upon
which we have only a negligible effect, if any.

Indeed, at the beginning of our esoteric practice, the
forms upon which we can have hardly any influence at all
constitute the greater part of what we can see. In fact, to
understand the nature of this group, we must observe
ourselves. Then we find out which forms we ourselves
are causing. We discover that it is what we ourselves do,
want, and so on that is expressed in these forms. They
manifest our instincts, desires, and intentions. Indeed,
our whole character is expressed by this particular world.
In other words, we find that our conscious thoughts and
feelings can influence all the forms in this higher world
that are not produced by us. But once the forms produced
by our being come into existence, we cannot influence
them.

To the eye of higher vision, a human being's inner life
displays itself in outer figures, just like other things and
beings. The inner world of instincts, desires and ideas becomes, for higher cognition, a part of the outer world. Just
as, when surrounded by mirrors in the physical world, we

can see our bodily form from all sides, so in a higher world we can see a mirror image of our soul being.

31. At this stage of esoteric development, we reach the point where we can overcome the illusion deriving from the narrowness of the personal self. Where before we regarded only what worked upon our senses as the outer world, now we can regard what lives inwardly, in our personality, also as an outer world. In this way we gradually learn from experience to deal with ourselves in the same way as we deal with the beings in the world around us.

32. If we were to see the spiritual worlds before we were sufficiently prepared for their nature, the picture of our own soul (as described above) would arise before us as a riddle. For in the spiritual world we are faced with the figures and forms of our instincts and passions in animal, or more rarely, human shape. Though the forms of these animals in the spiritual world are never quite the same as they are in the physical world, there is nevertheless a similarity between them. The unpracticed observer would probably find them identical. Therefore, as we enter the higher world, we must acquire entirely new ways of evaluating what we see. Furthermore, not only do things that belong to our inner life appear outwardly around us, but they also appear as mirror images of what they really are. Numbers, for instance, must be read in reverse: 265 really means 562. Similarly, we see spheres as though we were at their center, and then we must translate, as it were, this interior view. Soul qualities, too, appear in mirror images. For example, a desire for something external will manifest as a form moving *toward* the desiring person. And the

passions, which are seated in our lower nature, can take on the shapes of animals or animal-like beings hurling themselves upon us. In fact, of course, these passions are directed at the outside world. It is in the outer world that they seek the object that will satisfy them. In the mirror image, however, this seeking for satisfaction outside appears as an assault on the person harboring the passions.

33. Esoteric students who, before ascending to higher vision, have come to know their own character traits by calm, objective self-observation will find the strength and courage to act appropriately when they see the externalized mirror image of their inner being. But those who have not gained sufficient knowledge of themselves by such self-examination will not recognize themselves in their mirror-image and will mistake that image for a different, alien reality. Or the sight may frighten them and, because they cannot bear it, they may convince themselves that the whole thing is a fantastic figment, without consequence. Clearly, as both cases demonstrate, reaching this stage of inner development prematurely and without proper preparation can fatally impede one's further training.

34. In order to proceed further, it is essential to pass through the experience of spiritually seeing our own soul. For the soul and spirit beings we are best placed to understand are those which live within ourselves. If we have worked diligently in the physical world to acquire knowledge of our own personality, and we then immediately encounter its image in the higher world, we can compare the two. We can relate the higher phenomenon to one we already know and thus set forth from solid

ground. Otherwise, no matter how many other spiritual beings approach us, we would be unable to gain any understanding of their natures and special characters. Instead, we would soon feel the ground giving way beneath our feet. It cannot be emphasized often enough that the sure path to higher worlds leads through careful self-knowledge and the self-assessment of our own nature.

35. What we first encounter on the road to the higher worlds are thus spiritual *images*. This is because the reality to which these images corresponds lies within ourselves. Consequently, as students of the occult, we must be mature enough not to expect solid realities at this stage and to consider images as appropriate to our present level of contemplation. But within this world of images we can discover something new. Although our lower self comes before us only as a mirror image, our higher self appears in the middle of it in its true reality. Out of the image of our lower personality, the true form of the spiritual I becomes visible. From this spiritual I, the threads are then spun out to other, higher spiritual realities.

36. This is the moment to use the two-petalled lotus flower in the region of the eyes. Once this lotus flower begins to move, we are in a position to establish a connection between our higher I and higher spiritual beings. This is because the currents or streams emanating from this lotus flower move toward higher realities in such a way that we can be fully conscious of their movements. Indeed, just as light makes physical objects visible to our eyes, so these streams make the spiritual beings of the higher worlds visible to us.

37. It is by means of meditative absorption in the ideas of spiritual science which contain fundamental truths that students of the inner path learn to set in motion and direct the currents that stream from the lotus flower between the eyes.

38. At this point in our development, the value of sound judgment and a training in clarity and logical thought become especially evident. We need only bear in mind that the higher self—which until now has lain dormant within us, seedlike and unconscious—is here born into conscious existence. This birth is not just an image. It is a literal birth in an absolutely real sense: a birth into the spiritual world. And, if it is to be viable, the being that is born—the higher self—must enter this world with all its necessary organs and faculties. Just as nature must take care that infants are born with fully formed, healthy eyes and ears, so the laws of our own development must ensure that our higher self begins its conscious existence equipped with all the faculties it needs.

The laws that are instrumental in the development of our higher spiritual organs are none other than the sound laws of reason and morality in the physical world. Just as babies mature in their mother's wombs, so the spiritual human being develops within the physical self. And just as the health of a baby depends on the normal functioning of natural laws in the mother's womb, so the health of our spiritual humanity is likewise contingent on the laws of our ordinary understanding at work in our life on earth. No one can give birth to a healthy higher self who does not live and think in a healthy manner in the physical world. Living in harmony with nature and reason is the basis of all true spiritual development.

Just as a baby while still in its mother's womb already lives according to the forces of nature that its sense organs will perceive only after it has been born, so, in physical life, the human higher self already lives according to the laws of the spiritual world. And just as an unborn child, out of an obscure feeling or consciousness of life, makes use of the forces it needs, so we, too, can use the forces of the spiritual world before our higher self is born. Indeed, we *must* make use of these forces if our higher self is to enter the world as a fully developed being. It would be wrong, therefore, to think that we cannot accept the teachings of spiritual science until we can see for ourselves. For without immersing ourselves in such spiritual research we cannot attain any higher knowledge at all. To refuse to do so would be like a baby's refusing to use the forces available to it through its mother's body and wanting to wait until it could acquire them for itself. Just as the embryo dimly feels the rightness of what it is offered, so we can have a sense for the truth of the teachings of spiritual science, even before we become clairvoyant.

Relying upon the feeling for truth, and clear, healthy, many-sided, critical thinking, we can gain an insight into the teachings of spiritual science, even though we do not yet see spiritual realities. First, we must study the fruits of mystical knowledge: this prepares us for our own spiritual perception. If we became able to "see" spiritually without such preparation we would be like a child born with eyes and ears, but without a brain. The whole world of colors and sounds would be spread out before us, but we could form no connection with it.

39. What was convincing and obvious to us before, because of our feeling for truth, our intuition, and our reason, becomes firsthand experience for us at the level of spiritual schooling or discipleship just described. We now have immediate knowledge of our higher self. And thereby we learn to recognize that this higher self is linked with spiritual beings of a still higher order and forms a unity with them. Moreover, we see that our lower self also originates in a higher world. And we are shown that our higher nature outlasts our lower nature. Consequently, we ourselves can now distinguish our transitory part from our permanent self. In other words, we come to understand, by our own power of vision, the doctrine of the embodiment (or incarnation) of the higher self in the lower self.

It then becomes clear that we are part of a higher spiritual context, which determines our qualities and our destiny. We begin to understand the law of human life, namely karma. We realize that our lower self, which shapes our existence in the present, is only one of the many forms our higher being can assume. And in this way we realize that it is possible to work on the lower self from the perspective of the higher self in order to become more and more perfect. From this moment on, we become able to discern great differences between human beings with respect to their degree of perfection. We become aware that there are people more advanced than we are, who have reached levels that still lie ahead of us. It becomes clear, too, that their teachings and actions derive from inspirations from the higher worlds. We recognize that this is so from our own first glimpses of those worlds. Thus the expression "great initiates of humanity" now begins to take on concrete meaning for us.

40. The gifts that the student of the inner path receives by virtue of achieving this stage of development are these: insight into the higher self and into the doctrine of the embodiment or incarnation of this higher self in a lower self; insight into the law by which life in the physical world is regulated according to spiritual relationships—the law of karma; and finally, insight into the existence of the great initiates.

41. Therefore it is said of students who have reached this stage that they lose all doubt. Before, their faith was built on reason and healthy thinking, but now this faith can be replaced by complete knowledge and insight that nothing can shatter.

42. Religious ceremonies, sacraments, and rites give us outwardly visible images of higher spiritual processes. Only a person who has not yet fully understood the depths of the great religions can fail to see that this is so. Once we can look into spiritual reality, we can also understand the great significance of those outwardly visible actions. Then religious services themselves become an image of our relationship to the higher, spiritual world.

43. By reaching this stage of inner development, students of the spirit actually become new beings. They can now mature gradually to the point where, by means of

the currents of the ether body, they are able to control a still higher element—the element of life—and thereby achieve a great degree of freedom from the physical body.

CHAPTER 7

CHANGES IN
THE DREAM LIFE OF
THE ESOTERIC STUDENT

1. An indication that we have reached, or soon will reach, the stage of development described in the last chapter is the change that occurs in our dream life. Previously, our dreams were muddled and random. Now they begin to take on a more orderly character. Their images connect in a meaningful way, like the thoughts and ideas of waking consciousness. We begin to recognize lawfulness, and cause and effect in them.

At the same time, the *content* of our dreams also changes. Whereas our dreams formerly contained only echoes of our daily lives, and transformed impressions of our surroundings or our own bodily condition, the images we now see arise out of a world unknown to us before. At first, however, the general character of the dreams remains the same. That is, compared to waking consciousness, our dreams continue to express their content symbolically. Any careful study of dreams confirms this undeniably symbolic character. For example, we may dream that we have caught a horrible creature that feels unpleasant in our hands. Awakening, we find we have been clutching a corner of the blanket. The dream expresses this experience—not directly and unvarnished, but in a symbol.

Or we may dream that we are fleeing a pursuer and feel afraid. Waking up, we discover that we suffered palpitations of the heart while we were asleep. Again, if our stomach is filled with heavy, difficult-to-digest food when we fall asleep, this too can produce anxious dreams. Events occurring in our surroundings while we are asleep may similarly be reflected symbolically in dreams. The striking of a clock can evoke images of soldiers marching by to the beat of drums. Or the crash of a chair falling can stimulate a whole drama, in which the noise is symbolically reflected in the dream as a gunshot.

The more orderly and structured dreams that we begin to experience once our ether bodies have begun to develop retain this symbolic mode of expression, but they no longer reflect only events that are connected to our physical surroundings or bodily processes. For, as the dreams originating in physical reality become increasingly regulated, they begin to mix with images expressing conditions and events of another world. At this point, then, we begin to have experiences inaccessible to ordinary waking consciousness. But we should never for a moment believe that true mystics, if they experience something of this order in a dream, take such dream experiences as the basis for an authoritative account of the higher worlds. Such dream experiences should be viewed only as the first signs of higher development.

A further consequence of this development is that it soon becomes apparent that dream images no longer lie outside the guidance of our rational mind, but may be considered by this intelligence in as orderly and lawful a way as the ideas and sensations of waking consciousness. In this way the difference between the waking state and dream consciousness increasingly disappears. We begin to remain awake, in the full sense of the word, during our dream life; that is, we begin to feel ourselves lords and masters of our pictorial representations.

2. When dreaming we are actually in a different world from the one revealed to us by the physical senses. However, as long as our spiritual organs are undeveloped, we can form only a muddled idea of this world. Until then it exists for us only as much as the sensible world would exist for a being with only the most primitive, rudimentary eyes. This is why we usually see only images and reflections of daily life in this second world. We see these images and reflections because our soul paints the pictures of its daytime perceptions into the stuff of which the dream world is made.

In other words, we must realize that, in addition to our ordinary, conscious, daytime life, we also lead a second, unconscious life in this other dream world. We engrave or imprint everything we perceive or think onto this other world—but we can see these imprints only if our lotus flowers have been developed. These lotus flowers, of course, are always present in us, but only in a skeletal, undeveloped form. We cannot perceive anything with them in our waking state because the impressions made upon them in that state are very weak. The reason for this is similar to why we do not see the stars by day. Namely, their light is too weak when compared with the powerful light of the sun. In the same way, the weaker impressions of the spiritual world count for very little when compared to the powerful impressions of the physical senses.

When the doors of the outer senses are closed during sleep, these impressions from the spiritual world light up at random. As they do so we then become, as dreamers, aware of experiences in the other world. At first, of course, these experiences consist of no more than what the sense-bound mind imprints on the spiritual world. Only the development of the lotus flowers makes it possible to inscribe manifestations that do not belong to the physical world. Thereafter, complete knowledge of such inscriptions deriving from other worlds becomes possible with the development of the ether body.

This marks the beginning of our contact and communication with a new world.

We must now accomplish—by means of the instructions provided by esoteric training—a twofold task. First, we must become as conscious of what we observe in our dreams as we are of what we observe in waking life. Second, once we can do this, we must be able to carry this consciousness of dream observations into our ordinary waking state. In other words, our attention for spiritual impressions must be so developed that these impressions no longer vanish in the presence of physical impressions. Rather, we must be able to have both types of perceptions at the same time, side by side.

3. Once we have developed this faculty, certain elements of the picture described in the previous chapter appear before our spiritual eyes. From this point on, we can see that what exists in the spiritual world is the cause of what exists in the physical world. But within this spiritual world, we must first come to know our higher self.

Next, we must "grow" into this higher self. That is, we must consider it a real being and behave accordingly. This means that we immerse ourselves more and more in the idea and living feeling that our physical body and what we used to call our "self" are really only instruments of the higher I. In this way we begin to develop a relationship to our lower self that is like the relationship those who live only in the sense world feel toward their tools and vehicles. Just as we do not think of the car we drive as part of our I, even though we may say, "I drive" or "I travel," so the words "I go in through the door" now come to mean, for those who have developed themselves, "I take my body in through the door."

This idea must become so natural and obvious to us that we never for a moment lose our solid footing in physical reality. We must never allow any feeling of estrangement or alienation from the sense world to arise. To avoid becoming fantasists and fanatics, we must take great care that our experience of higher consciousness does not impoverish our life in the physical world, but enriches it.

4. Once we have begun to live in the higher I—or rather, even as we are in the process of acquiring such higher consciousness—we learn not only how to awaken the spiritual force of perception in the organ formed in the

region of the heart, but also how to control it, using the currents described in earlier chapters. This perceptive force consists of an element of higher materiality streaming out from this organ near the heart and flowing in shining beauty through the rotating lotus flowers and the other channels of the developed ether body. Thence it flows outward, into the spiritual world around us, making this world spiritually visible to us—just as the sunlight outside, falling upon objects from without, makes them visible to our physical eyes.

5. How this heart organ's force of perception is produced can be understood only gradually, during the process of inner training itself.

6. Not until we are able to direct this organ of perception through the ether body and into the outer world—so as to shine a light on the objects in it—can we see clearly the objects and beings of the spiritual world. It follows from this that perfect consciousness of an object in the spiritual world can arise only if we ourselves shed spiritual light upon it. In reality, the "I" that produces this organ of perception does not dwell within the physical body but outside it, as we have shown above. The heart organ is only the place where we kindle the spiritual light organ from the outside. Were we to kindle this light organ somewhere else, the spiritual perceptions produced would have no connection to the physical world. As human beings, however, our task is to bring higher, spiritual realities into relationship with the physical world. Humanity, indeed, is the means by which the spirit penetrates the physical realm. And the heart organ is precisely what the higher I

uses to make the sensory self its instrument so that it can use it.

7. When we have undergone the course of esoteric training described so far, the feeling that we experience for the things of the spiritual world becomes different from the feeling that ordinary, sense-bound human beings have for the physical world. The latter still feel themselves located in a particular place in the sense world, and the objects they perceive are viewed as being "outside." As spiritually developed persons, however, we now feel ourselves as if "united" with the spiritual objects we perceive, as if we were "inside" them. In other words, we wander from place to place in spiritual space. For this reason, spiritual science calls those at this level of inner development "Wanderers," for they are not yet at home anywhere.

Were we to remain mere "wanderers," however, we would find it impossible ever to truly define any object in spiritual space. Indeed, just as we define objects and places in physical space by starting from a given point of reference, so likewise if we wish to define things in spiritual space we must establish a similar reference point from which to begin. We must find a place in this other world, explore it thoroughly, and spiritually take possession of it. We must establish our spiritual homeland in this place, and then set everything else in relation to it. This is just what we do in the physical world. There, too, we view things from the perspective of the ideas and beliefs of our native country. A Berliner, for example, will describe London in a different way than a New Yorker will.

Yet there is a great difference between our physical and our spiritual homeland. We have nothing to do with the place of our physical birth, where we grow up and instinctively absorb various ideas and beliefs, which then involuntarily color everything we experience. Our spiritual home place is different. We create a spiritual home for ourselves in full consciousness. Therefore any judgment emanating from it is made in perfect, lucid freedom. In the language of spiritual science, this making of a spiritual home is called "Building a Hut."

8. At this stage of development, spiritual perception is initially limited to the spiritual counterparts of the physical world, insofar as these are present in the so-called astral world. This world contains all that is of a similar nature to human instincts, feelings, desires, and passions. In fact, every sense object in our physical environment has some spiritual force related to such human soul characteristics associated with it. A crystal, for example, flows into its form by means of forces that, to clairvoyant, higher vision, look like the instincts at work in human beings. Similar forces likewise draw the sap through the vessels of a plant, unfold its blossoms, and burst open its seed pods.

Just as objects of the physical world have form and color for our physical eyes, so too these supersensible forces can take on shape and color for those who have developed spiritual organs of perception. For example, if we have reached this stage, we can now see not only physically visible crystals and plants, but also the spiritual forces associated with them. Just as we see tables and chairs in the physical world, we can now see human and animal instincts—not simply manifested outwardly in behavior, but directly, as actual realities. Indeed, the entire world of instincts, drives, desires, and passions is now seen to form an astral cloud or aura enclosing every human being and animal.

9. In addition, as seers, we can now also perceive things that almost—or completely—elude our sensory grasp. For example, we can notice the astral difference between a room filled largely with people oriented toward lower things, and another containing those with higher aspirations. Not only is the physical atmosphere in a hospital different from that of a dance hall, the spiritual atmosphere is different as well. Similarly, a city that is a center of commerce does not have the same astral air as a university town. At first, of course, our capacity to perceive such things clairvoyantly is only weakly developed—just as our dream consciousness was weak in comparison with our waking consciousness before we began our inner work. Gradually, however, we mature and become fully awake on this level as well.

10. The highest attainment of a clairvoyant seer who has reached this stage of vision comes when the astral counter effect to human and animal instincts and passions is revealed. An action filled with love is accompanied by different astral phenomena than one arising out of hate. Meaningless desire produces an ugly astral counterpart or image, while the feeling for a high ideal creates a beautiful one. These astral counterparts are only faintly visible in physical life. Living in the physical world diminishes their strength.

For example, desire for something produces a counterpart in the astral world in addition to the immediate astral image of the desire itself. If the desire is satisfied and its object attained—or if there is at least the possibility of satisfying it—then (for the time being) the astral counterpart of the desire will be weak. It will achieve its full strength only after the death of the individual. At that point, the soul, in accordance with its nature, will still harbor the same desire but will now be unable to satisfy it, because it lacks both the object and the organs necessary to enjoy it.

If we are sensuously disposed in life, for instance, after our death we may still crave the pleasures of the palate. But we can no longer satisfy this craving; we no longer have a palate. The consequence is that our desire now produces a particularly powerful astral counterpart, which torments our soul. Such experiences, occurring after death in relation to these counterparts of our lower soul nature, are called "experiences in the soul realm," or more particularly, the "region of desire." They disappear only after the soul has purified itself of all desire for the things of the physical world. Only then does the soul ascend to the higher realm, the spiritual world.

Although these counterparts are only weak during our physical life, they nevertheless exist. They form our world of desires, accompanying us through life as a comet's tail accompanies its core. Thus they may be perceived clairvoyantly by seers who have reached a certain stage of development.

11. These and related experiences constitute the inner life of a student who has attained the stage of development

described in this chapter. To attain still higher spiritual experiences, we must ascend from this stage and climb yet further on the path.

CHAPTER 8

ACHIEVING CONTINUITY OF CONSCIOUSNESS

1. Human life unfolds in three alternating states. These are the waking state; the state of dream sleep; and the state of deep, dreamless sleep. To better understand how a person may attain deeper insights into the spiritual worlds, we must therefore form some idea of the changes that occur—for those seeking such knowledge—in each of these states.

Before we undertake the training required to attain such insights, our consciousness is continually broken by periods of sleep. During these intervals, our soul knows nothing either of the outer world or of itself. At certain moments, however, dreams—related either to events in the outside world or to the condition of our own body—rise up out of the ocean of unconsciousness. Normally, we consider such dreams as simply a particular manifestation of sleep, and hence generally distinguish only two states of consciousness: sleeping and waking. In occult science, however, the dream state has a separate significance, independent of the two other states.

The previous chapter described the changes that occur in our dream life when we undertake the ascent to higher knowledge. Our dreams lose their meaningless, disorderly, and disconnected character and begin to form an increasingly regular, lawful, and coherent world. As we evolve further, this new dream-born world not only becomes the equal of outer sensory reality with regard to inner truth, but also reveals facts depicting, in the full sense of the word, a higher reality. The sensory world conceals mysteries and riddles everywhere around us. At the same time it reveals the effects of certain higher realities in it. But as long as our perception is limited to our senses, we cannot penetrate to the causes of these effects. These causes are partially revealed to us in the state that develops out of our dream life—a state that by no means remains static.

Of course, we cannot consider these revelations to be real knowledge until we see the same things during our ordinary waking life. But with time and practice, this, too, occurs. That is, we evolve inwardly to the point of being able to transfer into waking consciousness the state we first formed out of our dream life. This enriches the sense world with something quite new. It is as if we were born blind and were to undergo a successful operation: we would find the world enriched by what our eyes then saw. It is the same when we become clairvoyant in the manner described above: we see the whole surrounding world filled with new qualities, new things, new beings, and so forth. Then we need no longer wait for dreams to live in another world. Now we can transpose ourselves into the state for higher perception whenever it is appropriate. In fact, this state now becomes as important to us as our active perceptions are in ordinary life when compared to what we perceive passively. Thus it may truly be said that, as students of the occult, we open the sense organs of the soul and behold things that must remain hidden from the physical senses.

2. This state, however, is only a transition to still higher stages of knowledge. For in due course, as we continue the practice of the exercises connected with our training, we find that the radical changes described above are not limited to dream life, but that this transformation in fact extends to what we had before considered the state of deep, dreamless sleep. At first we notice only that the complete unconsciousness that usually accompanies the state of deep sleep is occasionally interrupted by isolated conscious experiences. That is, out of the universal darkness of sleep perceptions of a previously unknown kind now emerge.

To describe these experiences is not easy. Our languages were designed for the material world and contain words that only approximate things not belonging to this world. Nevertheless, for the time being, we must use words to describe the higher worlds. But we can do so only if we make free use of analogy in much of what we say. We can do this because everything in the universe is related to everything else. Indeed, the things and beings of the higher and material worlds are sufficiently related so that—with a little good will—we can obtain a conception of the higher worlds through words intended for the material world. But we must always be conscious of the fact that a great part of such descriptions of the supersensible worlds must inevitably consist of analogies and symbols.

Only a part of esoteric training itself, therefore, uses ordinary language. For the rest, we learn a symbolic mode of expression that results naturally from our ascent into higher worlds. We acquire this language for ourselves during the course of our training. This does not mean, however, that we cannot experience something of the nature of the higher worlds from the exoteric descriptions given here.

3. The conscious—and, at first, isolated—experiences that emerge from the ocean of unconsciousness in deep sleep are best understood as a kind of "hearing." One may describe them as perceptible tones and words. Just as in comparison to ordinary sense experience we may describe what happens in dream sleep as a kind of "seeing," so we may compare what occurs in deep sleep to impressions received by the ears. (Incidentally, we may remark that in the spiritual worlds seeing is the higher of the two faculties. In the spiritual world, colors are higher than sounds and words. But what the student first perceives of this world as a result of esoteric training are not the higher colors but the lower sounds. It is only because our general development has already prepared us for the world revealed in dream sleep that we immediately see colors. We are less prepared for the revealing of the higher world in deep sleep. Therefore at first this world reveals itself only in sounds and words; and only thereafter does one ascend to colors and forms.)

4. Once we notice such deep sleep experiences, our main task is to make them as clear and vivid as possible. At first this will be very difficult, for we have only an extremely faint experience of what we perceive during this state. Thus, upon awakening, we may know that we have had certain experiences, but what these were remains still quite unclear. The most important thing at this early stage is to remain calm and composed. We must never for a moment yield to impatience and restlessness, for these are always harmful. Far from speeding up our development, they only delay and hinder it. In other words, we must calmly accept whatever we are given or granted and must never force anything. If, for a while, we do not notice any such experiences during sleep, we must simply wait patiently until they appear. This moment will assuredly come. Forcing their appearance may temporarily bring on such experiences, but then they may disappear again completely for longer periods of time. If we remain calm and composed, however, the ability to perceive these things will become our permanent possession.

5. Once this faculty for perception in sleep has been achieved, and sleep experiences stand before our consciousness in complete clarity and vividness, we can then focus our attention on them. We shall find that we are able to distinguish, with some precision, two kinds of experiences. The first is completely different from anything we have ever known. Initially it delights and uplifts us, but for the moment we should leave it alone. Such experiences, in fact, are the first heralds of a higher spiritual world in which we find our bearings only later.

Attentive observation of the second kind of experiences reveals a certain relationship between these and the ordinary world we live in. We find that these experiences illuminate not only our daily reflections but also the things around us that we have tried to grasp with our ordinary mind but could not. During the day we think about the world around us. We form mental pictures to try to understand the connections between things. We seek to understand what our senses perceive with the aid of concepts. It is to these mental pictures and concepts that this second kind of sleep experiences refers.

Concepts that were previously vague and shadowy now become resonant and alive, much like the sounds and words of the material world. We feel increasingly as though a higher world were softly whispering in our ears answers to the riddles we ponder. We find ourselves able to connect with our everyday life what we receive from the higher world in sleep. Things that we could only think about before now become as vivid and meaningful to us as any sensory experience in the physical world. We realize that the things and beings of this sense-perceptible world are more than what our senses can perceive. They are the expression and product of a spiritual world whose reality was hidden from us before, but now resounds for us out of our whole environment.

6. It is easy to see that, just as our physical senses are useful for the accurate observation of the world only if they are properly developed and structured, so this higher capacity of perception can benefit us only if the soul's newly opened organs of perception are in good order. As

indicated above, it is we ourselves who produce these higher senses by practicing the exercises that are part of our esoteric schooling. These exercises, of course, consist of concentration and meditation. Concentration means that we focus our attention on particular mental pictures and concepts connected with the mysteries of the cosmos. Meditation means living in such ideas, immersing ourselves in them in accordance with the instructions. Through such concentration and meditation we work on the soul and develop its organs of perception. Applying ourselves to the tasks of concentration and meditation, we help the soul to grow within the body, just as an embryo does within the mother's womb. The appearance of the isolated experiences that occur in sleep (as described above) signals the approach of the moment of birth for the soul that has now become free—for by this whole process the soul has literally become a different being, one we have germinated and brought to maturity within ourselves.

Great care must therefore be taken to ensure that we make the right inner efforts in concentration and meditation. The efforts must be precisely observed, for they are the laws governing the germination and development of the higher human soul being. When it is born, this higher being must be a harmonious, properly structured organism. If we neglect to follow the instructions carefully, the result will not be a true living being with its own inherent laws but a miscarriage on the spiritual plane, incapable of life.

7. Why the birth of this higher soul being must first occur during deep sleep becomes clear when we consider

that this delicate and vulnerable organism, lacking all powers of resistance, could not function if it appeared in physical everyday life, for the strenuous, harsh processes of this existence would overwhelm and overpower it. Its activities would be completely overshadowed by those of the body. In sleep, however, when the body and its activities based on sense perception are at rest, the activity of the higher soul, at first so delicate and inconspicuous, can make itself felt.

Here, again, we must bear in mind that we cannot consider these sleep experiences to be fully valid knowledge until we are capable of bringing the newly awakened higher soul across into waking consciousness. Once we can do this, we can perceive the spiritual world in its own character, between and within our everyday experiences. That is, our soul can grasp, as sounds and words, the mysteries of the world around us.

8. It must be understood that at this stage of esoteric training our experience is limited to spiritual experiences that are isolated, and more or less unconnected. Therefore we must guard against the temptation of using these experiences to construct a closed, systematic edifice of knowledge. Such attempts would only introduce all sorts of fantastic images and ideas into the soul world. We could easily construct a world that has nothing to do with the real spiritual world. Hence we must exercise the utmost self-discipline at all times. The best thing is to work on achieving greater and greater clarity regarding each experience, while at the same time waiting calmly for new experiences to arise spontaneously and to unite

themselves of their own accord with those already known.

In other words, we find ourselves experiencing, by means of the force of the spiritual world we have now entered, as well as by our continuing practice of the appropriate exercises, an ever-expanding extension of consciousness in periods of deep sleep. More and more experiences emerge from unconsciousness, our periods of unconscious sleep grow shorter and shorter, and gradually these isolated experiences come together of their own accord, without their real connection being in any way disturbed by such conjectures and conclusions as could derive only from the ordinary mind accustomed to the sense world. Clearly, the less we mix the ways of thinking appropriate to the sense world with these higher experiences, the better.

As we follow these guidelines, we draw ever nearer to that stage on the path to higher knowledge at which we can transform previously unconscious states of sleep life into full consciousness. Then, we will live in as real a world when our body is asleep as when we are awake. Needless to say, at first the reality we deal with when asleep is different from the sense-perceptible one in which our body lives. Eventually we learn—in fact, we *must* learn, if we are to keep our feet on the ground and not become fantastic visionaries—how to connect these higher sleep experiences with our ordinary, sense-perceptible surroundings. Nevertheless, at first, the world we experience in sleep is a completely new revelation for us.

Esoteric or occult science calls the important stage of development, wherein we become conscious in sleep, "continuity (or unbrokenness) of consciousness."[1]

9. For a person who has reached this stage of development, perception and experience are no longer interrupted by those periods when the body rests and the soul no longer receives impressions from the senses—consciousness is unbroken.

---

1. What is outlined here presents a kind of "ideal" for a certain stage of development, an ideal attained only at the end of a long path. As beginning esoteric students we first come to know only two states or conditions: consciousness in a state where previously only disordered dreams were possible, and consciousness in a state that previously we recognized as unconscious, dreamless sleep.

CHAPTER 9

THE SPLITTING
OF THE PERSONALITY
IN ESOTERIC TRAINING

1. In sleep, the human soul does not receive any information communicated by the physical senses. Perceptions from the ordinary outer world do not reach it. In fact, when we are asleep, our soul is in a sense outside that part of us, the so-called physical body, that mediates sense perceptions and thinking when we are awake. During this time, the soul is connected only with the subtler (ether and astral) bodies, both of which elude physical observation.

These subtler bodies do not cease their activity in sleep. The soul lives in a higher world, just as the physical body lives among the things and beings of the physical world, where it is affected by them and works upon them. But the soul's life continues during sleep. Indeed, the soul is particularly active then. However we can know nothing of our activity in this state until we possess the spiritual organs of perception necessary to observe—at least as well as our ordinary senses observe our physical surroundings in daily life—what goes on around us in sleep, and what we ourselves do there. As indicated above, esoteric training consists in the development of such spiritual organs of perception.

2. If our sleep life has been transformed by means of esoteric training along the lines described in the last chapter, then we can follow consciously all that goes on around us in that state. We can, at will, find our way in this new environment as easily as we can in our everyday waking life with our ordinary senses. We must bear in mind, however, that the perception of our ordinary sense-perceptible surroundings already requires a degree of clairvoyance. (This was pointed out in the previous chapter.) Still, at the beginning of our spiritual development we perceive things belonging to another world without being able to connect them with our everyday material surroundings.

3. These characteristics of sleep and dream life illustrate what is happening all the time in human beings. The soul lives and acts uninterruptedly in the higher worlds. From these worlds, the soul draws the inspirations and impulses by means of which it works unendingly on the physical body. This higher life remains unconscious in most human beings. But as esoteric students we bring these higher activities into consciousness. Thereby our lives are utterly changed. As long as our souls could not "see" in the higher sense, they were guided by superior cosmic beings. Now they have outgrown this guidance. Just as the operation that enables blind persons to see can change their lives so that they no longer need to be guided by others, so esoteric training likewise changes our lives.

As esoteric students, we outgrow the need to be led. From now on, we must lead ourselves.

As soon as this happens, of course, we become liable to errors of which ordinary consciousness can have no inkling. We now act out of the world from which, unknown to us before, higher powers once influenced us. These higher powers are regulated by the universal harmony of the cosmos. On the path of inner training, we move out of this cosmic harmony. We must now do by ourselves what was previously done for us without our help or participation.

4. For this reason esoteric writings often have much to say of the dangers connected with the ascent to higher worlds. These descriptive warnings may easily instill a fear of the higher life in timid souls. Yet it must be said that such dangers exist only if we fail to follow the necessary precautions. As long as we follow fully the advice given by true esoteric training, our ascent to higher worlds will endanger neither life nor limb, even though it will take us through experiences whose power and greatness exceed anything that our wildest sense-bound imagination could conceive of.

We encounter terrible powers that threaten life at every turn. We likewise learn to use certain forces and beings imperceptible to our physical senses. The great temptation will be to use these forces for our own, selfish, forbidden ends or to use them incorrectly out of an inadequate knowledge of the higher worlds. Some of these significant experiences, such as the encounter with the "guardian of the threshold," will be discussed in later chapters. Nevertheless, whether we are aware of them or not, we must realize that forces hostile to life exist. True, their relationship to us is determined by higher powers. But this relationship naturally changes when we consciously enter into the world previously hidden from us. At the same time, however, our own being is enhanced, and our horizon of life experiences is expanded tremendously. Real danger exists, however, only when impatience and arrogance lead us to assume a certain premature autonomy in regard to our experiences in the higher worlds: when we cannot wait for sufficient insight into the supersensible laws to be given to us. Clearly, in this domain, humility and modesty are far less empty words than they are in ordinary life. But if these qualities have become second nature to us in the best sense, then we can be certain that our ascent to a higher life will be without danger to what we call our life and health.

Above all, we must avoid any disharmony between our higher experiences and the events and demands of our everyday life. Our work is wholly here on earth. And if we evade our earthly tasks and try to escape into another world, we can rest assured that we will never achieve our goal. Yet what our senses perceive is only a part of this world. The beings who express themselves in the facts of the physical world are spiritual beings and inhabit the spiritual world. We must achieve and be blessed by the spirit so that we can introduce its revelations into the sense-perceptible world.

In other words, we must transform the earth by implanting in it what we discover of the spiritual realm. Our task is the transformation of the earth. Therein lies the only reason for seeking higher knowledge. The earth as we know it with our senses depends on the spiritual world, and this means that we can truly work on the earth only if we share in those worlds where creative forces are concealed. This realization should be our only motivation for wanting to ascend to higher worlds. If we enter esoteric training with this attitude and never deviate from the course it charts for us, we need fear no danger.

The prospect of potential dangers on the path of esoteric training should not keep us from following it; it should merely exhort us to work diligently on developing the qualities that every true student of esoteric knowledge should possess.

5. After these introductory comments, intended to dispel any fears, we shall now look more closely at some of these so-called "dangers."

Great changes definitely occur in the subtler (ether and astral) bodies of a person who undertakes esoteric training. These changes are connected with certain evolutionary processes taking place in the three fundamental forces of the soul: willing, feeling, and thinking. Before our training, the relationship between these is determined by higher cosmic laws. Nothing about the way we think, feel, or will is arbitrary. Every idea that becomes conscious is connected by natural laws to a particular feeling or act of will. For instance, when we enter a stuffy room, we open the window, or when we hear our name called, we answer the call. Similarly, a foul smell evokes a feeling of disgust in us. These seemingly simple connections between thinking, feeling, and willing are the foundation upon which, if we survey it, we find that our whole life is built. We even consider the interconnectedness of these powers of thinking, feeling, and willing—based, as they are, on the laws of human nature—to be a prerequisite for a "normal" life. We would consider a person who took pleasure in foul odors or refused to answer questions as "not normal," as violating the laws of human nature.

We expect a good upbringing and appropriate instruction to have results because we assume that we can connect a child's feeling, willing, and thinking in a way that corresponds to human nature. Thus we teach children certain concepts on the assumption that these will later connect with their feelings and will. All such efforts are based on the underlying fact that the midpoints of thinking, feeling, and willing are connected in our finer soul bodies in a definite and lawful manner.

This connection in the finer organism of the soul is reflected in the coarser physical body. Here, too, the connection between the organs of will and those of thinking and feeling is determined by laws. This is why a certain thought will regularly evoke a particular feeling or activity of will. In the course of higher development, however, the threads connecting these three basic powers are interrupted, severed. At first this break occurs only in the subtler soul organism, but later—as we continue our ascent to higher knowledge—the separation also extends into the physical body.

(In fact, as one develops spiritually, the brain actually separates into three distinct members. Admittedly, this separation is not physically perceptible to the ordinary sense organs and cannot be proven with even the finest physical instruments. Nevertheless, it occurs. Clairvoyants can see that the brain of a person possessing advanced abilities separates into three independently active entities: a thinking brain, a feeling brain, and a willing brain.)

6. At this point in our spiritual evolution, the organs of thinking, feeling, and willing function separately, quite independently of one another. Their interconnection is thus no longer regulated by their own inherent laws, but by the individual's awakened higher consciousness. Therefore one of the first changes we notice in ourselves as we advance in esoteric training is that neither ideas and feelings nor feelings and decisions are connected unless we ourselves create the connection between them. No impulse leads us from thought to action unless we ourselves freely create it.

Consequently we can now confront, dispassionately, events that before our training would have filled us with either burning love or bitter hatred. We can refrain from acting even in the presence of thoughts that would have spurred us automatically to action. Similarly, we can now act solely on the basis of pure will, even though others who have not undergone esoteric training cannot see the slightest reason for engaging in such actions. Thus the great accomplishment bestowed upon us on this path is the attainment of complete mastery over the interaction of our thinking, feeling, and willing. But such complete mastery over our soul forces also means that we have complete and individual responsibility for them.

7. Not until we have transformed our being in this way can we enter into a conscious relationship with certain supersensible beings and forces. For our soul forces (of thinking, feeling, and willing) are related to specific fundamental forces in the universe. For example, the force inherent in our will can affect certain things and beings of the higher world. It can also perceive them. But it can do so only once it has become free from its connection to feeling and thinking in our soul. As soon as this connection is undone, the activity of the will can be directed outward. The same is true of the powers of thinking and feeling.

If someone sends a feeling of hatred toward me, a clairvoyant can see this as a delicate cloud of light of a certain hue and can ward off this hatred just as we would ward off a physical blow that is aimed at us. Hatred thus becomes a perceptible phenomenon in the supersensible world. But we can see it only when we are able to direct the force inherent in our feeling outward, much as we direct the receptivity of our eyes outward into the sense world. And not only hatred, of course: other, more significant facts of the material world are also perceptible in the higher world. And one can enter into a conscious relation with these by discovering and liberating the basic forces of the soul.

8. Unless we follow the instructions of esoteric science closely, such a separation of thinking, feeling, and willing can easily lead us to deviate from the proper human path of development in three ways. Such a deviation occurs when the links connecting the three forces of the soul are

destroyed before higher consciousness and its under-standing are sufficiently advanced to be able to take the reins and lead the now separated forces in the right way to a free, harmonious working together. The achievement of higher consciousness is necessary because, as a rule, the three forces do not develop equally in every phase of a person's life. In one person thinking may be more devel-oped than feeling and willing, while in another feeling or willing may be predominant. As long as the connection between thinking, feeling, and willing remains regulated by the higher laws of the cosmos, however, such develop-mental discrepancies do not cause any disturbing irregu-larities in the higher sense.

If will predominates in a person, for example, then the cosmic laws ensure that other forces counterbalance it and keep it from becoming excessive. But once we begin esoteric training, then the regulating influence of feeling and thinking on the will ceases, and the will, now no longer held in check, constantly impels us on to tremen-dous performances of power. If we reach this point before we have mastered higher consciousness and are able to create harmony between our forces, then our will can run rampant. It can overwhelm us, so that our feeling and thinking sink into complete powerlessness and we be-come slaves, scourged by our will. As a result, we can be-come violent in character, rushing from one unbridled action to the next.

We can also go astray if our feeling frees itself from the restraint of higher cosmic laws. A person inclined to re-vere others, for instance, can then become so completely dependent on them that he or she loses the will and ability to think. Instead of higher knowledge, such a person's lot is the most pitiful inner emptiness and impotence. If the natural tendency of our feelings is toward piety and religious exaltation, on the other hand, we can fall into raptures of religious self-gratification.

A third evil arises when thinking predominates. This produces a contemplative nature, but one that is closed in upon itself and hostile to life. For a person of such a nature the world has meaning only insofar as it provides objects to satisfy a boundless desire for wisdom. Thoughts no longer stir such a person to action or feelings. Instead, such people become indifferent and cold, avoiding contact with ordinary things as if they were nauseating, or at least had lost all meaning.

9. Thus there are three ways in which we can go astray and deviate from the proper path of esoteric training. We can fall into willful violence, into sentimental luxuriating in feelings, or into a cold, loveless striving after wisdom. Viewed from the outside—by materialistic psychiatry, for instance—people who go astray in these ways do not seem very different, certainly not in degree, from those who are insane or at least extremely "neurotic." Naturally, esoteric training should not lead to such a condition. The important thing is to ensure that thinking, feeling, and willing—the three fundamental forces of the soul—have developed harmoniously before they are freed from the connection implanted in them and become subject to the awakened higher consciousness. If any mistake is made in this development and one of the three basic human forces

loses its restraint, then the higher soul's birth into existence will be a miscarriage. When this happens, unre-
strained force completely floods our whole personality,
and it will be a long time before balance can begin to be
restored.

Thus what seems a harmless aspect of our character before we enter esoteric training—such as whether we are
predominantly thinking, feeling, or willing types—is so
intensified once we become students that it can overpower the universal human element so necessary for life.
This only becomes a real danger, however, once we are
able to have conscious higher experiences in sleep consciousness as well as in the waking state. As long as our
experience of sleep remains at the level of the mere
awareness of the intervals in it, our sensory life, regulated
by universal cosmic laws, has a compensatory effect on
our soul when we are awake, restoring the soul's balance.

Hence it is critically important that our waking life be
normal and healthy in all respects. The more fully we can
respond to the demands that the outer world places on a
healthy, vigorous constitution of body, soul, and spirit,
the better. On the other hand, an overly exciting or ex-
hausting daily life can be harmful because we then add
potentially destructive and hindering influences to the
great transformations taking place in our inner life. We
should deliberately seek out situations for which our
strength is adequate and that can bring peace and harmony into our relationship with our surroundings. And
we should avoid everything that might disturb this harmony and bring anxiety and turmoil into our lives. Here it

is not so much a matter of getting rid of anxiety and turmoil in an outer sense as of taking care that our moods, intentions, and thoughts—as well as our physical health—remain stable and do not constantly fluctuate.

All this is not as easy for us after we have begun esoteric training as it was before. The higher experiences that now play into our lives continuously affect our whole existence. If anything is out of order in these higher experiences, then this irregularity lies in wait everywhere and can potentially throw us off at every turn. Therefore we must do all we can to ensure complete self-mastery. We should never lack presence of mind or fail to survey calmly all situations under our consideration. In fact, any true esoteric schooling itself develops all these qualities in us. In the course of such training, we learn of the dangers and, at the same time (and at the right moment) discover all the power we need to eliminate them from the field.

CHAPTER 10

THE GUARDIAN
OF THE THRESHOLD

1. Among the most important experiences in the ascent to higher worlds are the encounters with the so-called "guardian of the threshold." Actually, there are two such beings, not one. They are known as the "lesser" and the "greater" guardians. We meet the first when the connection between willing, thinking, and feeling in the finer (astral and ether) bodies begins to loosen. This was described in the previous chapter. The second, greater guardian is encountered when the separation of these three forces also affects the physical body, particularly the brain.

2. The lesser guardian of the threshold is an independent being, who does not exist for us until we have reached the appropriate level of inner development. Within the framework of this book, therefore, only a brief description of this guardian's essential characteristics may be given.

3. First, an attempt will be made to give a narrative description of the meeting with this guardian. It is only through this meeting, in fact, that we become aware that the implanted connection between thinking, feeling, and willing has been undone.

4. A thoroughly horrid, ghostly being stands before us. Hence we shall need full presence of mind and complete confidence in the safety and reliability of our cognitive path—which we have had ample opportunity to acquire in the course of our training—for this encounter.

5. The guardian then reveals the meaning of this moment in words, somewhat as follows:

Up to now, unseen by you, mighty powers presided over you. Through all the previous courses of your lives, they brought it about that every good deed was followed by its reward, and every evil action was followed by its grievous consequences. Through their influence your character was formed out of your life experiences and thoughts. They were the agents of your destiny. They determined, on the basis of your conduct in previous lives, the measure of joy and pain allotted to you in each of your incarnations. They ruled over you in the form of the all-embracing law of karma. These powers will now begin to loosen the reins by which they guide you. Now you yourself must do some of the work they did for you before.

Up to now, you endured many heavy blows of fate. You did not know why. Each was the consequence of a damaging deed done in a previous life. You found joy and happiness, and took these as you found them. These, too, were the result of earlier actions. You have many

beautiful sides to your character, and many ugly flaws.
You yourself produced these through your past experi-
ences and thoughts. Up to now, you were unaware of
this; only the effects were known to you. But the karmic
powers witnessed all your former actions and even your
most secret thoughts and feelings. And on that basis they
determined who you are now and how you live in your
present incarnation.

6. Now, however, all the good and bad aspects of your
past lives are to be revealed to you. You will see them for
yourself. They have been interwoven with your being all
along. They were in you, and you could not see them, just
as you cannot see your brain with your eyes. Now, how-
ever, your past actions are separating themselves from
you, stepping out of your personality. They are assuming
an independent form, one that you can see, as you can see
the stones and plants of the outside world. I am that self-
same being, who made a body for itself out of your good
and your wicked deeds. My ghostly form is spun, so to
speak, from the account book of your life. Up to now, you
have carried me invisibly within you. It was for your sake
that this was so. It meant that the hidden wisdom of your
destiny continued to work within you to eliminate the ugly
spots in my appearance. Now that I have come forth from
you, this hidden wisdom has also left you and will take
care of you no longer. Instead, it puts the work into your
own hands. I myself, if I am not to fall into corruption,
must become a perfect and glorious being. For, were I to
fall, I would drag you down with me into a dark, cor-
rupted world.

To prevent this, your own wisdom must be great enough to take over the task previously performed by the hidden wisdom now departed from you. I shall never leave your side once you have crossed my threshold. I shall always be there beside you in a form you can perceive. From then on, whenever you think or act wrongly, you will immediately see your fault as an ugly, demonic distortion in my appearance. My being will be changed and become radiantly beautiful only when you have made amends for all your wrongs and have so purified yourself that you become incapable of further evil. Then, too, I shall be able to unite with you again as a single being in order to bless and benefit your further activity,.

7. My threshold is built of every feeling of fear still within you and every feeling of reluctance in the face of the strength you need to take on full responsibility for your thoughts and actions. As long as you still harbor any trace of fear at directing your own destiny, the threshold lacks an essential element. As long as a single stone is missing, you will remain on this threshold, as if spellbound—or stumble. Therefore, do not try to cross this threshold until you are completely free of fear and feel yourself ready for the highest responsibility.

8. Until now, I have left you only when death called you from an earthly life. But, even then, my form was veiled from your eyes. Only the powers of destiny presiding over you could see me. During the interval between death and rebirth, based on my appearance, they formed in you the forces and faculties to enable you to work to make me beautiful in your next life, and so ensure the well-being of your progress. Thus it was I and my imperfections that made the powers of destiny send you back to a new earthly incarnation. When you died, I was there. It was for my sake that the rulers of karma decided that you must reincarnate. If, without knowing it, you were to transform and perfect me through life forever renewed in this way, then you could avoid falling into the powers of death. But then you would have become completely one with me, and, united, we would pass into immortality.

9. So now I stand visible before you, as I have always stood invisible beside you in the hour of your death. Once you have crossed my threshold, you will enter realms you otherwise entered only after physical death. Now you will enter them in full knowledge. From now on, though living outwardly and visibly upon the earth, you will live at the same time in the realm of death, that is, in the realm of eternal life. Indeed, I am your angel of death. But at the same time I also bring you never-ending higher life. While still living in the body, you will die through me and experience rebirth into indestructible existence.

10. In the realm you are henceforth entering, you will meet beings of a supersensible kind. Bliss will be your share in this realm. Yet I, I who am your own creation, must be your first acquaintance in this world. Earlier, I lived on your life. But now, through you, I have awakened to an independent existence of my own and stand before you as the visible standard of your future actions—and perhaps also as a constant reproach. You have been able to create me and in so doing have taken on the duty of transforming me.

11. What is indicated here in narrative form must not be understood only symbolically. It is, on the contrary, in the highest degree an absolutely real experience, which any student pursuing esoteric training to the appropriate level can have.[1]

12. The guardian's function is to warn us not to go any further unless we feel strong enough to meet the challenges contained in the words addressed to us. Horrid as it may be, the guardian's appearance is, after all, but the consequence of our own past lives. It is only our own character, awakened to an independent life outside of us.

This awakening of our character to an independent existence occurs as our thinking, willing, and feeling begin to separate. It is already a deeply meaningful experience to feel for the first time that we have given birth to a spiritual being. The whole purpose of our preparation—our esoteric training— is to enable us to bear the awful sight of

---

1. As is clear from the above explanations, the guardian of the threshold described here is an astral appearance that reveals itself to our newly awakened higher perception. Spiritual science guides us to this supersensible encounter. To make this guardian physically visible is an act of low magic based on the creation of a cloud of fine substance, a vapor mixture of several substances in a certain proportion. The developed forces of the magician can then give this vapor form and shape and animate it with our still unredeemed karma.

However, if we have sufficiently prepared ourselves for higher perception, we no longer need such sense-perceptible props. On the other hand, if we confront our unredeemed karma without adequate preparation, we risk going badly astray. Thus, we should not seek this encounter until we are really ready. Bulwer-Lytton's novel *Zanoni* contains a fictional representation of this guardian of the threshold.

this guardian without any trace of fear or aversion. When we meet the guardian we must feel our strength so grown that we can take upon ourselves the task of the guardian's transformation and enhancement in full knowledge and consciousness.

13. As a result of passing the meeting with the guardian of the threshold successfully, our next physical death is a quite different event than before. Dying becomes a conscious experience for us in which we lay aside our physical body, like a garment that is worn out or so torn that it is no longer usable. In a sense, our physical death will then upset only those close to us whose outlook and perceptions are still limited to the material world. In their eyes we "die," but nothing important changes for us in our surroundings. For before we die the whole supersensible world that we enter with death is already open to us—and after dying it remains open to us as before.

The guardian of the threshold is also connected with something else. Each of us belongs to a family, a people, a race. Our activity in this world depends upon our belonging to such a unit. Even our individual personality is related to it. In fact, our membership in a family, a nation, or a race affects not only our conscious activities, for every family, nation and race has its own destiny, just as each has its own particular character. As long as our perspective is limited to the material world, however, such realities remain merely general concepts. Materialistically biased thinkers regard with contempt any esoteric scientist who attributes family or national characteristics, and lineal or racial destinies to beings whom they consider just as real as the individuality to whom they attribute personality and destiny. Yet such esoteric scientists have come to know *worlds* of which our individual personalities are parts, just as our arms, legs, and head are parts of our body.

The life of families, nations, and races is affected thus not only by the individuals who belong to them but also by "family souls," "nation souls," and "race spirits." These are real beings. In a sense, as individuals, we are only the instruments—the executive organs, so to speak—of these "family souls" and "race spirits." Indeed we may say, for example, that the soul of a nation or people makes use of the individuals who belong to it to accomplish certain tasks. This "folk soul" does not descend to the sense-perceptible world: it remains in the higher realms. To work in the physical world, the folk soul of a nation makes use of individual human beings as physical organs. This process is analogous, on a higher level, to a civil engineer in the material world making use of construction workers to execute the details of a project.

In the truest sense, we each receive our allotted human task from our family, nation, or race soul. As long as our experience is limited to the sense-perceptible world, we are not initiated into the higher purpose of which this task is a part, but work unconsciously toward the goals of our group souls. As soon as we encounter the guardian of the threshold, however, we not only know our own personal tasks but also have to work consciously to help accomplish those of our people and our race. Thus, each expansion of our horizon also extends the sphere of our responsibility.

The actual process underlying this revelation at the threshold is the adding of a new body to our subtler body. This is much like putting on a new garment. Previously we moved through the world clothed only in the sheaths that envelop our personality. Higher spirits, making use of our personality, oversaw what we had to do for our community, our nation, and our race. Now, however, the guardian of the threshold reveals to us that these spirits will no longer take care of us—from now on they withdraw their guiding hands. We must therefore leave behind all belonging to communities. Yet, as isolated individuals, we would wholly harden within ourselves and fall into ruin if we did not acquire the powers inherent in the spirits of our race and nation.

While many people certainly believe they have freed themselves fully from all tribal and racial connections and are simply "human" and nothing else, we have to wonder what made this freedom possible for them. After all, were they not given their place in the world by their family, and have not their lineage, nation, and race made them what they are? Their lineage, nation, and race have taught and educated them. They owe their ability to transcend tribal and racial prejudices to this education; lineage, nation, and race have enabled them to become the light-bearers and benefactors of their tribe or even their race. Thus, even though these people claim to be no more than "simply human," they owe the ability to make such claims to the spirits of their communities. In fact, only when we follow the path to inner knowledge will we experience what it really means to have left behind all tribal, national, and racial connections and to be abandoned by the spirits of nation, tribe, and race.

Indeed, it is on the esoteric path that we first experience for ourselves the meaninglessness of the education—for the life we are now entering—that all these connections have given us. For as soon as the threads joining willing, thinking, and feeling begin to snap, all that has been instilled in us completely dissolves. We then look back upon the results of our previous upbringing as if we were watching our house crumble into individual bricks that we must then rebuild in a new form.

It is much more than a mere figure of speech when we are told that, after the guardian begins to speak, a whirlwind arises from the place where the guardian stands, extinguishing all the spiritual lights that illuminated our life up to now. Utter darkness then surrounds us, broken only by the radiance streaming from the guardian. Out of this darkness we hear the guardian exhorting us: *Do not cross my threshold until you fully understand that you yourself have to illuminate the darkness before you. Do not take a single step forward until you are absolutely sure that you have enough fuel in your own lamp—because the lamps of those who have guided you up to now will no longer be there in the future.*

Following these words, we must turn and cast our gaze behind us. The guardian of the threshold now pulls aside the curtain that hitherto veiled life's deep mysteries from us. Now the spirits of tribe, nation, and race are revealed in their full reality. We see clearly how we have been guided in the past and that now this guidance is no more.

This is the second warning we receive at the threshold from its guardian.

14. No one could bear the sight described here without preparation. The higher training that enables us to reach the threshold helps us at the same time to find the necessary strength when we need it. In fact, our training can proceed so harmoniously that when we enter this new life we do so without drama or tumult. Our experiences at the threshold are then accompanied by a premonition of that bliss which will be the keynote of our newly awakened life. The sensation of our new freedom outweighs all other feelings. And in the light of this sensation, our new duties and responsibilities seem natural and inevitable at our given stage of life.

CHAPTER 11

LIFE AND DEATH:
THE GREAT GUARDIAN
OF THE THRESHOLD

1. The previous chapter showed that the significance of the encounter with the so-called lesser guardian of the threshold lies in the fact that in this meeting we perceive a supersensible being that we ourselves have, to some extent, created. For the body of this being is made up of the results—previously invisible to us—of our own actions, feelings, and thoughts. Unbeknownst to us, these invisible powers became the causes of our destiny and personality. And from this moment on, we realize how we ourselves laid the foundations of our present life in the past. In this way, our own being begins to become transparent to us.

For example, certain tendencies and habits dwell within us. Now, we realize why we have these. We have met with certain strokes of fate. Now, we recognize where these come from. We understand why we love some things and hate others, why some things make us happy and others cause us unhappiness. That is, we come to understand our visible life on the basis of its invisible causes. Even the essential facts of life, such as illness and health, birth and death, are unveiled before our sight. We realize that we wove the causes that led us to return to life before we were born. We come to know, too, the being within us that is created but unfinished in this visible world—the being that can be finished and perfected only in this same visible, perceptible world. For the opportunity to work on the completion of this being does not exist in any world other than this.

Thus we recognize that death cannot permanently separate us from this world. Inwardly, we realize,: "Once I entered this world for the first time because I am a being who needs life in this world in order to acquire qualities I cannot acquire in any other world. And I must remain connected to this world until I have developed everything within me that can be found there. One day, because I have acquired all the faculties I need in this sense-perceptible, visible world I shall become a useful coworker in another world."

In other words, one of the most important experiences we gain from initiation is that we learn to know and to treasure the true value of the visible, sense-perceptible world better than we could before our esoteric training. Indeed, only through insight into the supersensible worlds do we realize the value of the sense-perceptible world. A person who has not experienced this insight and thus perhaps believes that the supersensible regions are of infinite, incomparable worth, may underestimate the sense-perceptible world. But those who have had insight into the supersensible know that without their experiences in the visible world they would be quite powerless in the invisible worlds.

To live in the invisible worlds, we must have the tools and faculties appropriate to them. We can develop these only in the visible world. For example, if we are to become aware of the invisible worlds, we must learn to "see" spiritually. This power of spiritual vision in a "higher" world develops only gradually by means of experiences in the "lower" world. A person can just as little be born with spiritual eyes in a spiritual world, if he or she has not previously developed these eyes in the sensible world, as a child could be born with physical eyes if these had not been developed in the mother's body.

2. We can now understand why the "threshold" to the supersensible world is protected by a guardian. For under no circumstances could we be allowed a true insight into these realms if we had not first developed the necessary faculties. And this is the reason why—if we have not yet developed the ability to work in other worlds—a veil is drawn across our experiences when we die and enter these realms. That is, we may not behold the supersensible worlds until we are ready and mature enough to do so.

3. When we enter the supersensible worlds, life takes on a completely new meaning for us. We see that the sensible world is the fertile soil—the living medium or substratum—of a higher world. Indeed, in a certain sense, this "higher" world seems incomplete without the "lower" one. Two vistas then open up before us—one into the past,

the other into the future. We see into a past in which this physical, sensible world did not yet exist. The prejudice that the supersensible, spiritual world developed out of the sensible, material world lies far behind us now. We know that the supersensible world came first and that the sensible, physical world developed out of it.

We see that before we entered the physical world for the first time we ourselves belonged to a supersensible world. And that this supersensible world too had to pass through life in the sensible world in order to develop further. Its further evolution was impossible unless it passed through the physical realm. Indeed, only if certain beings evolved with the appropriate faculties in the physical realm could the supersensible realm advance in its evolution. We are those beings. Human beings, as we are today, arise at a level of spiritual existence that is incomplete, imperfect. Within this level we are in the process of being led to a stage of completion that will enable us to continue our work in the higher world.

At this point, our vision turns toward the future, revealing a higher level of the supersensible world. Here we find fruits first formed in the sense-perceptible physical world. The sense world we know today will have been overcome by then, but its results will have been incorporated into a higher world.

4. We can now begin to understand the meaning of illness and death in the physical world. Death, after all, merely expresses the fact that the supersensible world had previously reached a point beyond which it could not advance by its own efforts. Universal death would have

overtaken it if it had not received a new life-impulse. This new life has become a struggle against universal death. Out of the ruins of a withering, inwardly solidifying world, the buds of a new world blossomed. That is why our world contains both death and life—and why things are gradually intermingling. The dying parts of the old world still cling to the seeds of the new life developing out of them. We can see this most clearly expressed in ourselves. The sheath we bear has been preserved from the old world, but the seed of the being that will live in the future is already growing within it.

Hence, as human beings, we have a double nature: mortal and immortal. Our mortal being is in its final stages, our immortal being is only beginning. But only within the twofold world, mortal and immortal, whose expression is the sense-perceptible physical world, can we acquire the faculties that will lead the world to immortality. Our task is to harvest from the mortal world fruits for the immortal. When we contemplate our being, which we ourselves have built up in the past, we must say to ourselves: "We bear within ourselves the elements of a dying world. These elements work within us. Yet gradually, with the help of the new immortal elements awakening within us, we are able to break their power." In this way, our path takes us from death to life.

Indeed, if we were conscious in the hour of our death, we would realize: "The dying world was our teacher. The fact that we die is a result of all the past with which we are interwoven. But the field of mortality has prepared seeds of immortality for us. We carry these with us into another world. If everything depended only on the past, we would never have been born. The past—its life—ends with birth. Life in the sensible world is wrested from universal death by the new seed of life. The time between birth and death is simply an expression of how much the new life can wring from the dying past. And illness is but the consequence of the part of this past that is dying."

5. Here we find an answer to the question, "Why must we work our way only gradually from error and imperfection to truth and goodness?" Our actions, feelings, and thoughts begin under the rulership of what passes and dies away. Out of what passes away, our perceptible physical organs evolve and are fashioned. As a result, these organs and all that stimulates them are doomed to perish and die away. We will not therefore find anything immortal in our instincts, drives, and passions, nor in the organs belonging to them. We will find immortality only in what appears as their product, in the work done by these organs. Only when we have drawn out of this perishable world all that there is to be drawn out of it will we be able to cast aside the foundation we have outgrown, which manifests itself in the physical-sensible world.

6. Thus the first guardian of the threshold replicates our dual nature as human beings, consisting of mixed mortal and immortal elements. And thereby this guardian clearly reveals to us what still needs to be done to attain the sublime light-form capable of dwelling again in the world of pure spirit.

7. The first guardian makes graphically clear how entangled we are with the physical, sensible world. This

entanglement is expressed, first of all, by the presence of instincts, drives, passions, egotistic desires, and all forms of self interest. It manifests, too, in our belonging to a race, a nation, and so forth. Peoples and races are, after all, merely different developmental stages in our evolution toward a pure humanity. The more perfectly that individual members of a race or people express the pure, ideal human type—the more they have worked their way through from the physical and mortal to the supersensible and immortal realm—the "higher" this race or nation is.

Human evolution, through repeated incarnations in ever "higher" nations and races, is thus a process of liberation. In the end, we must all appear in harmonious perfection. We perfect ourselves likewise as we pass through ever purer moral and religious convictions. For every stage of moral development still harbors some yearning for what is perishable, as well as idealistic seeds of the future.

8. What the lesser guardian of the threshold shows us are only the results of time that has passed. The seeds of the future are present only to the extent that they have been woven into the guardian in the past. But human beings are called upon to bring with them into the future supersensible world all that they can gain from the material world. Were we to bring with us only what was woven into our image from the past, we would accomplish only a part of our earthly task. That is why, after a certain period of time, the lesser guardian of the threshold is joined by a greater guardian. What takes place in the form of this meeting with the second, greater guardian will once again be described in narrative form.

9. After we have recognized in the lesser guardian those things from which we need to free ourselves, a magnificent form of light comes to meet us on the path. The beauty of this form is difficult to describe in ordinary language. The meeting takes place when our physical organs of thinking, feeling, and willing have so separated from each other—and even from the physical body—that they themselves no longer regulate their mutual interaction. Instead, higher consciousness, now detached completely from physical conditions, regulates their relations. As a result, our organs of thinking, feeling, and willing have become instruments under the control of the soul, which exercises its rulership from the supersensible realms. The soul, freed in this way from all sensory bonds, now encounters the second guardian of the threshold, who speaks somewhat as follows:

10. *You have freed yourself from the world of the senses. You have earned the right of citizenship in the supersensible world. From now on, you may work from there. For yourself, you no longer need your physical bodily nature in its present form. If all you wanted was to acquire the capacity to dwell in the supersensible world, you would never need to return to the world of the senses. Look at me. See how immeasurably I am raised above all that you have already made of yourself up to now. You have reached your present stage of completion by means of faculties that you were able to develop in the sense world while you were still dependent upon it. Now you are entering a time when the powers you liberated must continue to work upon this sense world. Until now, you have*

worked only to free yourself, but now that you are free, you can help free all your fellow beings in the sense world. Up to now, you have striven as an individual. Now you must join yourself to the whole, so that you may bring with you into the supersensible realm not only yourself, but also all else that exists in the sensible world.

Some day, you will be able to unite with my form, but I myself cannot find perfect blessedness as long as there are others who are still unfortunate! As a single, liberated individual, you could enter the realm of the supersensible today. But then you would have to look down upon those sentient beings who are not yet freed. You would have separated your destiny from theirs. But you are linked together with all sentient beings. All of you had to descend into the world of the senses to draw from it the powers required for a higher world. Were you to separate yourself from your fellow beings, you would misuse the powers you were able to develop only in consort with them. If they had not descended into the sense world, you would not have been able to descend either. Without them, you would lack the powers you need for supersensible existence. You must share with the others the powers that you achieved with them.

Therefore I refuse to admit you to the highest regions of the supersensible world until you have used all your powers for the deliverance of your fellow world and fellow beings. What you have already achieved entitles you to dwell in the lower regions of the supersensible world. But I will stand at the doorway to the higher regions "like the cherubim with the flaming sword before the gates of

Paradise." I will deny you entry as long as you still have powers that you have not put to use in the sense world.

If you do not use your own powers, others will come who will put them to use. Then a high supersensible world will incorporate all the fruit of the sensible realm, but the ground you stand on will be pulled out from under your feet. The purified world will develop over and beyond you. You will be excluded from it. If this is your choice, then yours is the black path. But those from whom you separate yourself tread the white path.

11. In this way the great guardian of the threshold announces his presence soon after the meeting with the first guardian. Initiates now know precisely what awaits those who yield to the temptations of a premature stay in the supersensible realms. The second guardian of the threshold emits an indescribable radiance. Union with this guardian is a distant goal for the beholding soul. Yet the certainty is also present that such a union is possible only after all the powers that have flowed into us from this world have been expended in the service of liberating and redeeming it.

Should we therefore decide to meet the demands of this higher being of light, we will be able to contribute to the liberating of the human race. We will then offer up our gifts and talents on the sacrificial altar of humanity. But if we prefer our own premature ascent into the supersensible world, then the stream of humanity will pass over and beyond us. Once we have liberated ourselves, we can no longer win any new powers for ourselves from the world of the senses. If, therefore, we still place our work at the disposal of the sense world, we do so knowing that we are thereby renouncing any gain for ourselves from the place of our future effort. But even when the choices are presented so clearly, it cannot be said that taking the white path is a matter of course. What we choose, after all, depends on whether we have sufficiently purified ourselves of all traces of selfishness, so that at the time of making the decision the allure of personal salvation and blessedness no longer tempts us.

This temptation of personal salvation on the "black" path is the greatest we can conceive of. The white path, on the other hand, does not seem tempting at all. It does not appeal to our egotism. What we receive in the higher regions of the supersensible realms, when we take the white path, is not something for ourselves, but only something that flows from us, namely, love for the world and our fellow beings around us. But on the black path nothing that our egotism desires is denied us. On the contrary, the fruit of this path is precisely the complete satisfaction of egotism. Thus those seeking salvation only for themselves will almost certainly choose the black path. In their case, indeed, it is appropriate.

Clearly, therefore, we must not expect occultists on the white path to provide any instructions for the development of our egotistic I. They have no interest whatsoever in the bliss and salvation of the individual. As far as a white occultist is concerned, each one of us must attain such salvation for ourselves. It is not their task to accelerate this process. What matters to them is the evolution and liberation of *all* beings—human beings *and* their fellow beings. Therefore their task is only to indicate how we can train our powers for collaboration in this work. Thus they place selfless dedication and the willingness to sacrifice above all other virtues. Nevertheless, they reject no one outright, for even the most egotistic can purify themselves. All the same, those seeking only for themselves— as long as they do so—will get nothing from such occultists. Even though true occultists will never refuse to help a seeker, such seekers may well deprive themselves of the fruit of their helping guidance.

Therefore if we truly follow the instructions of a good esoteric teacher we will understand the demand that the second guardian makes after we have crossed the threshold. Indeed, if we fail to follow such a teacher's instructions we cannot expect ever to reach the threshold at all. The instructions of true esoteric teachers lead to the good, or they lead to nothing. To guide us to egotistic salvation and mere existence in the supersensible world is not their task. On the contrary, their task, from the start, is to keep us at a distance from the supra-earthly world until we can enter it with a will dedicated to full and selfless collaboration.

The path to supersensible cognition indicated in this book leads to a soul experience. It is particularly important that anyone aspiring to this level of experience harbor no illusions or misunderstanding regarding this experience. Certainly, it is easy to deceive ourselves about these things. One of the gravest deceptions occurs when the entire realm of soul experiences spoken of in spiritual science is misclassified so that it appears placed in the same category with superstition, visionary dreams, mediumism, and other aberrations of the natural human striving for the spirit. This error occurs most often when students following the path presented here are confused with others who in their attempt to find a way into supersensible reality deviate from authentic *cognitive* striving, and so decline into the aberrations mentioned above.

If we follow the path presented here, our soul experiences take place within the realm of pure soul-spiritual experience. In order to have such experiences, we must first make ourselves as inwardly free and independent of physical life as we are, in ordinary consciousness, when we form *thoughts* about the perceptual world or our inner wishes, feelings, and intentions—thoughts that are independent of, and unattributable to, the actual experience of perceiving, or feeling, or willing. Some people, of course, deny the existence of such thoughts. They claim that we cannot think anything that is not drawn from perception or from inner life as this is conditioned by the body. Therefore, they say, all thoughts are simply shadow images of perceptions or inner experiences. Those who assert this, however, only do so because they themselves have never been able to develop in their souls the faculty of experiencing the pure, self-sufficient life of thought. Once we have experienced this, and it is a living experience for us, we *know* that whenever thinking presides in our soul life we are engaged, to the extent that such thinking permeates our other soul functions, in an inner activity in whose creation the body plays no part.

In our ordinary soul lives, thinking is almost always mixed with other activities, such as perceiving, feeling, willing, and so on. These other activities originate in the body. But thinking plays into them. And, to the extent that it plays into them, something occurs in and through us in which the body has no part. Those who deny this cannot rise above the illusion caused by the fact that thinking is always observed together with these other activities. With inner effort, however, we can experience in our souls the thinking part of our inner life *in itself*, apart from all the other activities of our inner life. That is, we can isolate something consisting only of pure thoughts from everything else in our soul life. These thoughts are self-sustaining and free of any admixture of other activities; they have been cleansed of everything resulting from the perception of the outer world, bodily functions, or the inner life they govern. By their very nature, in and of themselves, such thoughts show themselves to be spiritual, supersensible entities. If our soul unites with these thoughts, and excludes all perception, remembering, and other inner activities, it lives with this thinking in the supersensible realm, that is, it experiences itself outside the body. Once this is understood, it can no longer be doubted that the soul can have supersensible experiences outside the body, for this would mean denying what we know from firsthand experience.

Why, we may wonder, are people reluctant to accept this confirmed fact? The reason is that it does not reveal itself unless we have first put ourselves in the soul state capable of receiving it. People, however, are generally suspicious if they are required to make an effort of a purely soul nature for something to be revealed to them that in itself is independent of them. They believe that because they have to prepare themselves for its revelation, they have actually produced its content by themselves. In other words, for the most part, people prefer to have passive experiences that require no effort on their part. If, in addition, they are also unfamiliar with the most basic requirements for a scientific understanding of a set of facts, they will easily take the contents or products of a soul in a state of lowered consciousness—that is, a state below the degree of conscious activity displayed in sensory perception and voluntary action—as an objective revelation of a non-material reality. In other words, they will mistake visionary experiences, mediumistic revelations, and similar soul contents for true spiritual perception. What is experienced in such states of lowered consciousness, however, is not a *super*sensible but a *sub*sensible world.

Not all conscious waking life runs its course wholly within the body. In particular, what is most conscious in waking life takes place on the boundary between the body and the outer physical world. Hence what happens in our sense organs during perception is as much the projection *into* the body of an event occurring outside, as it is a permeation of this outer event *by and from* the body. Likewise, our will life is based upon the fact that human nature is embedded in the cosmic whole so that what happens in us through our will is also simultaneously a part of the whole cosmic process.

These soul experiences that occur at the boundary of the body certainly depend to a great extent on our human bodily organization. At the same time, however, the activity of thinking plays a part in these experiences. And the more it does so, the more our sensory perception and willing become *independent* of the body. Visionary experiences and mediumistic demonstrations, on the other hand, depend completely on the body. In such practices everything is eliminated from soul life that could make perception and willing independent of the body. As a result, the contents and products of the soul become nothing more than manifestations of the physical life of the body. Visionary experiences and mediumistic phenomena, in fact, result from the fact that in them a person is *more* dependent on the body than in ordinary perception and willing. True supersensible experience, on the other hand, such as described in this book, requires that we

direct our development in the opposite direction from
that of visionary and mediumistic experience. In other
words, we strive to make the soul progressively less dependent on the body—more independent of it—than it is
in ordinary perceiving and willing. Thereby we achieve
the degree of independence from the body that is characteristic of pure thinking, thus extending the range of our
soul activities.

To develop supersensible soul activities as intended
here, it is most important that we penetrate the experience
of pure thinking clearly and consciously. Indeed, this experience of pure thinking is already and fundamentally a
supersensible activity of the soul—although it is one in
which we do not yet perceive anything supersensible. In
pure thinking, we are already living in the supersensible
realm; but at this point it is still only pure thinking, and
not yet anything else, that we experience in a supersensible way. Further supersensible experiences must then be
a continuation of the soul experience we have achieved in
union with pure thinking. Therefore, it is crucial that we
experience this union correctly, for right understanding of
this union sheds the light of insight on the nature of supersensible knowledge.

On the other hand, as soon as our soul life sinks below
the clarity of the consciousness experienced in thinking,
we stray from the right path to true cognition of supersensible worlds. Instead, our soul is taken over by our bodily
functions, and what it conveys to us will be a revelation
not of the supersensible but merely of events occurring in
our body in the realm below the sense-perceptible.

．　．　．

As soon as our soul experiences enter the realm of the supersensible, they are no longer as easy to describe in ordinary language as experiences in the material world. Therefore, when reading or hearing descriptions of the supersensible world, we must be mindful that the language employed is, in a way, further removed from the actual facts than is the case when we talk about physical experiences. We have to understand that many expressions and terms employed in these descriptions are, as it were, only images delicately hinting at what they refer to.

It was stated in the first chapter that "originally, all rules and teachings of spiritual science were presented in a symbolic sign language;" and the third chapter likewise spoke of a certain "system of writing" or "occult script." From this it may appear that such a language or script may be learned in the same way as we learn the letters and combinations of an ordinary language in the physical world. Certainly it is true that there have always been, and still are, schools and associations of spiritual science possessing the symbolic signs by which supersensible facts may be expressed. A person initiated into the significance of these signs therefore possesses a means of directing his or her soul experiences to the supersensible realities in question. What is much more important, however, is that in the course of such experiences—as a soul can attain through realizing the contents of this book, for instance— the soul should find this script revealed through its *own* contemplative experiences of the supersensible.

The supersensible realm speaks to the soul, which must then translate what it has heard into symbolic signs in order to survey it in full consciousness. What is communicated in this script can be realized by every soul. In the course of this realization—a process the soul controls, as we have indicated—the results described in this book become evident.

• • •

Readers should approach this book as though they were having a conversation with the author. Therefore the advice about receiving personal instruction on the path to higher knowledge should be understood to refer to this book. In the past, there were good reasons for restricting personal instruction to oral teaching. Now, however, we have reached a stage of human development when spiritual scientific teaching and knowledge must be spread abroad much more widely than ever before. Its teachings must become much more accessible than they were in the past. For this reason the book must take the place of oral instruction.

The belief that we need personal instruction in addition to what is said in this book is true only to a limited extent. Some of us may indeed need some additional personal help, and such further instruction may be helpful and meaningful to the individuals concerned. But it would be wrong to think that anything of importance has been left out of this book. Everything may be found in this book if only we read it properly and, above all, completely.

• • •

Some of the descriptions in this book may seem to call for a complete transformation of our whole being. However, read rightly, these descriptions do no more than indicate the state of soul necessary for those moments in our lives when we encounter the supersensible world. For such moments, we develop this state as a kind of second being within us, while our other healthy self continues on its normal course. We learn to keep the two beings apart and to regulate their interaction properly. All this we do in full consciousness. Thus we do not become useless and incompetent in practical life; we do not lose our interest and skillfulness for life because we are "practicing spiritual research all day." Nevertheless, the experiences we have in the supersensible world will radiate throughout our whole being; rather than alienating us from life, they will make us more productive and effective.

The descriptions in this book had to be presented as they were because each process of cognition directed toward the supersensible world takes our whole being. Every moment that we are given over to cognition of supersensible realities engages us totally. Perceiving a color, for example, requires only the participation of our eyes and the related nerves. But our whole being participates in the perception of supersensible things. Our whole being becomes, in a sense, "all ears" or "all eyes." This is the reason why information on how to develop supersensible cognition often seems to imply a complete transformation of our being, as though our ordinary being were wrong and must become different.

• • •

I would like to add a few points to what was said in chapter 6 concerning the effects of initiation. With slight modifications this holds good also for other sections. Some readers may wonder why supersensible experiences are described in pictures and images, rather than abstractly, as ideas. The reason is that, to experience supersensible reality, it is important that we know ourselves as supersensible beings in a supersensible world. We become aware of the reality of our own supersensible nature in the descriptions of the "lotus flowers" and the "ether body." To enter the supersensible realm without such an awareness of our own supersensible nature would be like being aware of the events and processes of the physical world that surrounds us, but not of our own bodies. Just as we become conscious of ourselves in the physical world through the perception of our physical body, our own supersensible form, which we can perceive in our "ether body" and our "soul body," makes us conscious of ourselves in the supersensible realm.

The first decades of the twentieth century brought with them momentous accomplishments in science, art, and spiritual life. During these same years, Rudolf Steiner sought to address the need for a modern spiritual practice—one standing fully within the flow of contemporary life that might produce the insights needed by individuals and communities to meet the practical and personal demands of the age. In proposing a path of self-development, a teacher can only speak of what he knows and is master of. Such was certainly the case with Rudolf Steiner.

Parallel with his university training in the natural sciences and philosophy in Austria, and his outer life as a scholar and editor, Rudolf Steiner cultivated a contemplative life of extraordinary depth and clarity. From childhood on he had had personal experiences of the supersensible, but it was only after many years of disciplined inner work that he felt that the secure foundations had been created for what he called Anthroposophy, or a "science of the spirit." Only then did his own spiritual maturity reach the point where he could share publicly the results of his spiritual researches.

Beginning in 1901, when he was forty years of age, and continuing until his death in 1925, Rudolf Steiner presented the fruits of his inner work in lectures, articles, and books. *How To Know Higher Worlds* dates from this early period, first appearing in book form in 1909. Although complete in itself, Rudolf Steiner viewed this work from the outset as part of a larger whole that was to include not only a second volume on meditation, but also many other aids in support of the meditative life. While the planned second volume never appeared in the form originally intended, innumerable lectures, essays, and meditative verses did appear. In addition, personal consultations were given and an Esoteric School was established. In other words, Rudolf Steiner made sure that, at every stage of an aspirant's development, both personal and communal supports were available, yet always in a way that left the student entirely free.

This motif of freedom is central to the structure and content of *How To Know Higher Worlds*. In the first chapters, Rudolf Steiner leads the reader carefully through a series of exercises that steady the soul, while leaving it free and opening it to new experiences.

He then goes on to relate the exact nature of the changes that take place within the meditant as a consequence of this self-development, and also to describe the inner experiences a student can expect to have along the path. Having completed the book, the reader understands not only the exercises and moral injunctions associated with the meditative path, but also their consequences. The end as well as the means are presented together.

Fully informed from the beginning concerning the effects of meditation, we can therefore choose freely whether or not we wish to embark upon a spiritual practice. Rudolf Steiner viewed this as a requirement for modern spirituality: namely, that individual freedom and judgment be respected at every point.

In earlier times, students of spiritual knowledge worked intimately with those who had already trodden the path of initiation. The sacred traditions of the past often required the student to give over his or her being to the directives of a master or guru. Today, such subservience is inappropriate. Teachers still exist, but our relation to them should now be based on mutual respect and freedom. The teacher can offer counsel, but the student must, in the end, judge for himself or herself whether to accept the advice and how to implement it. Still, the question justifiably arises, how can I best determine my own particular meditative path?

Rudolf Steiner gives important suggestions in this regard in the prefaces to *How To Know Higher Worlds*. A student, having worked for a time with particular exercises, can detect the effects these have on the soul. From the very beginning, therefore, it is important to develop a sense for one's own soul health, for the benefit or detriment arising from each exercise. Choosing from the many suggestions for meditation offered by Rudolf Steiner, each student can then shape his or her meditative practice according to whatever need is felt, working with those exercises that strengthen the weaknesses that are apparent, and harmonize those areas of soul life that are in turmoil.

Although Rudolf Steiner did give personal advice concerning self-development, he emphasized that "a totally *direct* relationship with the objective spiritual world is more important than a relationship to the personality of a teacher" (Preface, p. 9). In addition, he reassured the seeker that help was always available when truly needed. It may come in the form of written material or oral teaching, and also through persons who are our companions in spiritual striving. Today we learn from each other, as well as from masters. Through shared study and struggle, we begin to think and feel anew.

This process of transformation can lead to one's becoming a member of a community of meditants. From his earliest years, Rudolf Steiner worked not only publicly, but also more quietly with a circle of serious students. In 1923, with the refounding of the Anthroposophical Society, this intimate work took on a new form: the First Class of the School of Spiritual Science. Those already familiar with Steiner's anthroposophical teachings and ready to enter into a more serious meditative life within the community of Anthroposophy could apply to the First Class. To them, Rudolf Steiner gave special teachings in the form of imaginations leading toward the threshold of the spiritual world and beyond. Thus he provided not only a text, but a human community, in support of the meditative life.

How To Know Higher Worlds offers an introduction to the inner life and to an inner discipline that can heal and transform us profoundly.

I will turn now to a more detailed consideration of the book's contents.

• • •

There are many reasons that can lead one to begin a meditative practice, but at the outset every true aspirant must pass through the "portal of humility." We may be drawn to the inner life because of suffering, loss, or grief, in the hope of finding solace. Certainly nothing is wrong, and much is right, with this, and techniques exist that can help with every kind of personal trial. Yet every step inward should be joined to a gesture outward. We are safeguarded from becoming self-absorbed in our own concerns by mindfulness of the suffering of others. Our mastery of personal hardships is achieved not by withdrawal from the world. Rather we retreat so that we can better serve. This is part of the practice of humility.

The same steadfast commitment to selflessness should be present at every stage along the path, from the first attempt at meditation to the experience of enlightenment. This commitment to selflessness forms the moral foundation for all spiritual self-development—whether concerned with stilling our rage or opening the eyes of the soul that reveal the spiritual dimensions of all creation. Always, whatever is done is done in service. If anything, Rudolf Steiner states the point even more forcefully:

> Let nobody imagine that he or she gains any advantage over fellow human beings by developing clairvoyance, for that is simply not so. One makes no progress that can be justified on any ground of self-interest. One achieves progress only

insofar as one can be more useful to others. The immorality of egoism can find no place in the spiritual world. A person can gain nothing for him or herself through spiritual illumination. What one does gain is gained only as a servant of the world in general, and one gains it for oneself only by gaining it for others.

(*Background to the Gospel of St. Mark*, p. 18)

The "portal of humility" stamps our striving with the seal of reverence for all of life and with a devotion to truth and service. These form the fundamental mood of soul for one's meditative life. If we cultivate this mood, we have already taken a significant step on the path of meditative life.

Every sound spiritual practice begins with moral development. This is as true of Buddhism and the mystical traditions of Christianity as it is of Anthroposophy. In keeping with this, the opening pages of *How To Know Higher Worlds* strive to engender in us the tenor of soul that should underlie meditation. It is an attitude of selfless love. Esoteric schooling never has as its goal the accumulation of spiritual treasures for personal gain. If one seeks for oneself, one actually achieves nothing. Every striving, every accomplishment is properly placed only when it is placed at the service of others. Once the context of selfless love is established, meditative practice can unfold within it.

•   •   •

The first chapter of *How To Know Higher Worlds* stands like a microcosm, reflecting in its few pages the entire path of spiritual development. Having begun with the creation of a moral foundation for meditative practice, we pass on to the care of the soul, to harmonizing and healing. The peace thus achieved permits the unfolding of a higher self, which can turn away from personal matters to the universal spiritual realities surrounding us. In what follows, as well as in other writings, Rudolf Steiner offers us a wealth of additional details concerning each stage of the path from Preparation through Illumination to Initiation. Nevertheless, if we wish to penetrate fully the path Steiner suggests, we can do no better than to ponder more and more closely the first chapter of *How To Know Higher Worlds* where we find the several stages of the path reflected in miniature.

Once we have established the inner axis of veneration for all that is noble, as well as the attitude of service, we are ready to begin our work with the soul. Special times are set aside for regular practice. During these we undertake exercises that can work deeply into our essential nature, unraveling the knots of destiny and quieting the turmoil of life.

Turning inward in meditation, we often feel beset, if not overwhelmed, by the troubles and crises of daily life. The first task, therefore, is what I call "soul hygiene." At this point, we are not concerned with the attainment of higher knowledge, but simply strive for the tranquility and self-control required for subsequent stages of self-development. These exercises can begin with reflection on a past, perhaps difficult personal experience. Through such quiet reflection we gradually come to distinguish the important from the unimportant in what we have experienced, and to view the problem or issue from a higher, calmer vantage point.What before might have thrown us into turmoil is now beheld with equanimity.

As a consequence of these exercises, one's inner life no longer swings from one extreme to another and, in the resultant calm, one can begin to sense the dawning of a "higher self." The experience of this moment is one which can center a student's entire life—inner and outer. With the first modest success in bringing the buffeting forces of life under control, one can already sense a firm inner ground on which to stand. Time and again, one needs to step out of the work-a-day tempo and create one's own private time for contemplation. As with all such exercises, repetition is the key. Even after an initial success, one needs to return repeatedly to that higher ground which is open to the calm, clear air of the spirit.

We need not fear that we will be estranged from life as a consequence of this accomplishment, far from it.We are able to consider life all the more deeply because personal passions have been set aside, and we begin to learn what only compassion can teach.

Essential though they are, the path of reverence and the exercises concerned with "soul hygiene," just described, form only the preliminary stages of meditative life to which others can now be added. In particular, while these foundational exercises are intended to foster a mood of reverence, bring tranquility to the soul, and give birth to a

higher self, subsequent exercises foster other soul capacities that lead us from our own concerns to an ever deep-
ening understanding of what is universally human.

The exercises concerned with this second stage of the
meditative path allow everything of a personal nature to
fall away. In contemplating an appropriate verse, man-
tram, or image, the meditator moves from personal issues
to eternal ones. The specific choice for the focus of meditation may be recommended by a teacher, or selected
from the treasures available from past masters of the inner
path. Working with such material is like lifting our gaze
from the ground on which we stand to the infinite horizon.
We come to sense a "living world of silent thought activity" around us. This vibrant, luminous, circling stream
carries us into its creative glories. The world's wisdom
lights up as a stream of thinking. This is a dawning experience of the spirit, an experience of the Logos. We feel
the touch of the divine, although at first only gently and
without understanding. Before insight can be joined to experience we will need to pass through many experiences
and confront numerous trials. Like a child newly born
into a strange and beautiful world, we must mature. Impressions must unite with understanding for meaning to
arise. Both impressions and thinking must be raised from
the earthly to the divine.

• • •

Whether we are occupied with its opening or final
pages, Rudolf Steiner's other writings and lectures extend

and develop in innumerable ways the themes introduced in
How To Know Higher Worlds. For example, in a lecture
given on December 27, 1911, Rudolf Steiner elaborates on
the path of reverence, the foundation for everything that
comes afterward, described in chapter one. But where before only a single mood of soul was described, Steiner now
identifies four stages along the way. Elsewhere, he speaks
of the "mission of reverence," and so on. One can pause at
any place in Steiner's works and uncover a wealth of material suitable for a lifetime of practice. This is as it should
be, for no single spiritual exercise can ever be exhausted.
Rather, each exercise leads us deeper and deeper, offering
us not only a fount of personal renewal, but also a basis for
right work in the world. By faithfully embracing the meditative life, we move daily through domains of inner experience that transform the soul into a beautiful, selfless
organ for collaboration in the redemptive work taught by
the Buddha and exemplified by the Christ.

The teaching of humility and compassion, in fact,
frames the whole of *How To Know Higher Worlds*. We
are enjoined at the beginning to start our meditative life
under the sign of humility, and likewise at the end of the
book, when we stand before the Great Guardian, we are
asked to take a vow of compassion.

*Up to now, you have striven as an individual.
Now you must join yourself to the whole, so that
you may bring with you into the supersensible
realm not only yourself but also all else that exists
in the sensible world* (p. 203).

Thus, our work is not done even when we have achieved full enlightenment. Rather must we continue to care for the needs of others, for all our companions on the Earth. The deeply Christian-Bodhisattvic character of the entire book is as much a part of the teaching as the specific indications for the exercises. It is an integral part of the practice.

$$\cdot \quad \cdot \quad \cdot$$

In *How To Know Higher Worlds* and elsewhere, Rudolf Steiner gives many exercises whose purpose is to prepare the soul for challenges quite different from those that arise during the course of our sense life. Perhaps the most important are those aimed at developing the six soul qualities essential for a healthy and balanced life within the supersensible.

These qualities are important because many of the supports provided by the sense world vanish when the aspirant crosses the threshold into the spiritual world. It is, therefore, especially important to strengthen one's own inner resources and soul stability early on, and to maintain those resources. Steiner gives six "accessory exercises" which can be practiced by the student regardless of what other meditative work has been undertaken. These establish the requisite inner balance. Neglecting the accessory exercises is dangerous. Therefore Steiner warns us that, "All meditation, concentration, or other exercises are worthless, indeed, in a certain respect actually harmful, if life is not regulated in accordance with these conditions" (*Esoteric Development*, p. 102).

The six conditions are the development of: 1) clarity of thought, 2) mastery of the will, 3) equanimity of feeling, 4) positivity, 5) openness, and 6) the establishment of harmony among these five. The student begins in each case in the simplest possible way. For example, clarity of thought can best be strengthened by taking a common object (a tack, pencil, or whatever) and holding it before the mind's eye unswervingly for five or ten minutes. No thought should enter that is not connected directly with the object under consideration. Time and again, the mind will wander, and time and again we will need to return our attention to the task. Gradually the experience arises that we can control our attention. Our attention, which before flitted without notice from one subject to the next, has been steadied and brought under our control. The remaining five exercises can likewise be pursued for a month each, always using the simplest means. Then one can begin again.

As we faithfully execute these and similar preparatory exercises, soul capacities are cultivated which lead to the first experiences of a supersensible kind. What is the character of these initial experiences? Although the path for every individual is unique, certain characterizations can be helpful, especially as false expectations often allow the real promptings of the spirit to pass by unnoticed.

Frequently, one expects the spiritual to appear in the form of visions or hallucinations, but these are not the stuff of authentic spiritual experience. Such experiences may indeed arise, but they are more a manifestation of our own selves than of higher worlds, and it is essential to find one's proper relationship to them. In many passages, Rudolf Steiner turns us away from visionary or mediumistic experience toward more subtle but reliable intimations of the spirit. He writes, for example, that "one of the gravest deceptions occurs when the entire realm of soul experiences spoken of in spiritual science is misclassified so that it appears placed in the same category with superstition, visionary dreams, mediumism, and other aberrations of the natural human striving for the spirit" (Epilogue, p.207).

Rather than visions, Steiner points to the deep importance of a responsive yet disciplined life of feelings. Instead of trying to "see" into the spiritual world, we should attend to the inner feelings that accompany our meditation. Concerning spiritual imaginations, Steiner writes,

> One must let the pictures weaving in the soul become, as it were, spiritually transparent in oneself by continuous activity. They will gradually become so through their own development. In fact, they will become such that one no longer "beholds" them, but only feels them living in the soul and perceives the substance of supersensible reality through them.
> (*The Threshold of the Spiritual World*, p. 170)

Even when writing about auric colors, Steiner is careful to point out that, by such colors, the genuine spiritual seer means something quite specific: namely, "that he or she encounters something experienced in soul *that is like* the perception of that particular color in sense experience." By contrast with this, those who hold that what they experience is "the same as the color in the sense world are not spiritual students, but visionaries or people with hallucinations." The spiritual world is not an ethereal, hazy double of the physical sense world, but reveals itself to our heightened sensibilities in quite other forms.

Steiner often elucidates the difference between sense experience and the supersensible by reference to memory. To the eye, the objects of the sense world appear in a certain way. But our memory of the same experience is not the same as the initial sense experience. A memory of childhood may be vivid, but it differs from the actual experience in significant ways. Supersensible experience is much like memory, except that it refers to no past sense impression, but rather to present soul and spiritual aspects of our world.

For example, as we continue our practice, a tranquil openness of soul can be established in which a specific mood arises. Perhaps one is working with budding plants on the one hand and dying ones on the other, as described in Chapter Two. The experience of new life brings with it a definite feeling, one that is delicate but objective; the same is true of the experience of the dying plant. Each produces a "quite definite form of feeling." That is, a feeling arises with a very specific shape or form. It is these clear feelings that we should hold to. Thereby our feeling life gradually becomes schooled, and an entire universe of soul experience of the world around and within us dawns in us. In some individuals these feelings provoke actual color images, in others not. In either case, however, what is important is not the image itself (usually simply borrowed from the sense world) but what shines through as a "form of feeling." Only through the latter can we be led on to the spiritual beings who stand beyond.

In this way, *How To Know Higher Worlds* provides the student with a systematic path for the cultivation of the feeling life so that it can become truly cognitive, the basis for genuine knowledge. To further this end Rudolf Steiner recommends exercises that move the student inwardly through the mineral, plant and animal kingdoms to the experience of the human being. At each stage a new range of soul experience is added, and a rich and trustworthy inner language is forged in the process.

To begin with, the supersensible often appears in brief encounters: it is gone as soon as it has arrived. Ordinary memory is insufficient to hold it. Yet, as we continue to meditate, we notice many changes in our inner life and come to acknowledge the potent reality of the spirit, now known through firsthand experience. Our dream life, for example, previously chaotic or determined by the day's events, gradually takes on a more ordered form. When awakening, we sense a different character and relation to sleep—for the development of the spiritual bodies, as these are affected by meditation, naturally leads to a transformation of dream life. In sleep, when the proddings of the sense world are silenced, the first clear intimations of the spirit show themselves. It is essential to treat these experiences as provisional, and not to attempt to interpret them prematurely. Many further stages must be passed through before reliable spiritual insights can be had by the meditant. Still, with each step along the way the link between the spiritual in us and the world grows stronger and stronger.

• • •

The path set forth in *How To Know Higher Worlds* is not a linear one, uniformly applied and graded step-by-step. Everyone will find their own unique way and pace of development, meet trials specific to themselves, and make discoveries that only they can make. Rudolf Steiner's own advice varied depending on the audience to whom he spoke. When lecturing to a group of scientists and scholars he recommended they begin their practice with thought exercises. To a group in Scandinavia he elaborated a path leading through color and tone to inner moods and from there to an experience of the etheric world. He gave special mantric material to doctors, to teachers, to priests and so on. Entering a cathedral we all stand first in the nave, but then we may well find our way to a small side chapel dedicated to a particular saint. Likewise when we set out upon the meditative path we may quickly find our way to a practice appropriate to our needs.

Yet over and above the variety of spiritual practices is an architecture whose form is dictated by the requirements of our age. Every culture and every age has a means of connecting with the divine. We are well aware that the range used today extends from shamanic drumming to yoga, from sweat lodge to prayer, from psychedelics to asceticism. What is appropriate for our present age and for me? At the time Rudolf Steiner was writing the explosion of practices had just begun, and was especially centered on those discovered by Europeans in Asia. How can we understand the relationship between the way described in *How To Know Higher Worlds* and these others, for example to those that employ breathing exercises? Concerning this Rudolf Steiner wrote:

> All the exercises described in the book [*How To Know Higher Worlds*] are the spiritual correlate suited to the West, of that for which the Orient longs: to bring the rhythm of the process of breathing into the process of cognition. If our thinking had the same tempo as our breathing many secrets of the universe would be disclosed to us.
>
> (*The Karma of Materialism*, p. 36)

In other words, Rudolf Steiner lifts to the level of cognition, to our seeing and reflecting, all that which is enacted with the breath in ancient breathing exercises. In cognition, too, there is a process of exchange between the inner world and the outer. In order to know our universe we both take in and move out—we breathe light, as Steiner called it. Cognitive practice, therefore, is a yoga not of breathing in the element of air, but of breathing through all our senses in the element of light.

This is one approach to the question of the relationship of Rudolf Steiner's description of the spiritual path to that given in other traditions. Another centers around the

Christ event, the Mystery of Golgotha and its significance for our meditative life. Indeed, Rudolf Steiner's entire effort can only be understood within the context of that event. He sought, often in unspoken ways, always to work out of the forces that flowed into world evolution through the deed of the Christ. *How To Know Higher Worlds* is no exception.

Finally, Rudolf Steiner felt it his task to create a way to the spirit that met the specific demands of Western culture in the twentieth century. Ours is a time deeply shaped by developments in science and technology, and Rudolf Steiner himself was trained as a scientist and engineer, before he turned to philosophy and literature. His path to the spirit reflects this striving to meet the expectations of the modern soul, to respect its demand for freedom and its need for a clear, articulate knowledge of the spiritual— one which could be put to good use whether in medicine, education or farming. While deeply respectful of Eastern spiritual paths, and of the variety possible within individual spiritual practice, Rudolf Steiner sought to delineate a safe, sure way to the spirit that was at the same time both deeply Christian and completely contemporary, a path committed to loving service and to uncovering the deepest truths to which we are granted access. At one point Rudolf Steiner described Anthroposophy as a path from the spiritual in us to the spiritual in the universe. *How To Know Higher Worlds* can be our first guide along that path. We will discover other guides as the need arises.

. . .

Related Reading

Also by Rudolf Steiner:

Anthroposophy in Everyday Life
Anthroposophical Leading Thoughts
Anthroposophy and Christianity
Anthroposophy and the Inner Life
A Road to Self Knowledge
At the Gates of Spiritual Science
Calendar of the Soul, The (verses through the year)
Effects of Spiritual Development, The
Esoteric Development, (selected lectures)
Fruits of Anthroposophy
Inner Development of Man, The (a lecture)
Learning to See into the Spiritual World
Metamorphosis of the Soul, Paths of Experience, (2 volumes)
Outline of Esoteric Science, An (chapter 5)
On the Life of the Soul
Paths to Knowledge of Higher Worlds
Prayer
Secrets of the Threshold
Self-Transformation (selected lectures)
Stages of Higher Knowledge, The
Threshold of the Spiritual World, The
Theosophy, (chapter 4)
True and False Paths in Spiritual Investigation

All works by Rudolf Steiner that are in print are available from the Anthroposophic Press, 3390 Route 9, Hudson, NY 12534. A free complete catalog is published annually. For out of print works, write: Rudolf Steiner Library, 65 Fern Hill Road, Ghent, NY 12075.

By other Authors:

Kühlewind, Georg. *From Normal to Healthy*. Hudson, N.Y.: Lindisfarne Press, 1988.

—— S*tages of Consciousness*. Hudson, N.Y.: Lindisfarne Press, 1984.

—— *Working with Anthroposophy*. Hudson, N.Y.: Anthroposophic Press, 1992.

Lievegoed, Bernard. *Man on the Threshold*. Stroud, England: Hawthorn Press, 1985.

Rittelmeyer, Frederick. *Meditation: Guidance of the Inner Life*. Edinburgh: Floris Books, 1987.

Schiller, Paul Eugen. *Rudolf Steiner and Initiation*. Hudson, N.Y.: Anthroposophic Press, 1981.

Smit, Jörgen. *How to Transform Thinking, Feeling and Willing*. Stroud, England: Hawthorn Press, 1989.

—— *Meditation: Bringing Change into Your Life*. Sussex, England: Sophia Books, Rudolf Steiner Press, 1996.

Tomberg, Valentin. *Inner Development*. Hudson, N.Y.: Anthropsophic Press, 1992.

physical world, 196-200; soul's attention to, 39-40; transcending in initiation, 196; transcending in meditation, 36; visualizing in exercises, 59-60; *See also* incarnation; life

decisions, reasoning process for making, 112-113; severed from feelings, 178; *See also* ideas; thoughts

decisiveness, power of, 79-80; *See also* indecisiveness; self-confidence

deeds. *See* actions

delusion. *See* illusion; fantasy

desire, affect of in higher worlds, 77; affecting training, 96, 102, 129; astral expression of, 63, 158-160; exercises for perceiving, 62-63; experienced after death, 160; expressed in forms, 142, 143; expressed in soul organism, 109; as force in animals, 49; projection of, 143-144; renouncing, 76, 85, 87; *See also* feelings; instinct; pleasure

destiny. *See* fate

destructiveness, avoiding, 104, forces of, 115, 182

development. *See* evolution; growth

deviation, occurring in esoteric training, 179-180

devotion, affecting soul, 18, 22; enhancing search for higher knowledge, 18, 86; training in, 19, 21

directions. *See* exercises

discrimination. *See* judgment

divine, personal experience of, 23; *See also* God

dogma, absent in esoteric training, 106

doubt. *See* fear

dream sleep state, relationship of to waking state, 162-163

dreamless sleep state, relationship of to waking state, 162-164

dreams, changes in, 151-163; consciousness maintained in, 153, 154, 162-173, 182; evolutionary development of, 151-152; *See also* sleep

duties. *See* responsibilities

E

earth, spiritual foundation of, 176; *See also* outer world

education. *See* knowledge

egoism, black path appealing to, 205; refraining from, 23; *See also* I; self

embodiment. *See* incarnation

empathy, experiencing through sounds, 45-46; *See also* sympathy

endurance, balanced with heart, 101; cultivating, 121, 138; *See also* strength

enjoyment. *See* pleasure

environment, effect of on dreams, 152; affect of on spiritual exercises, 92; analyzing needs of, 101; astral expres-

eyes, chakra of, 145, 146; relationship of to spirit eye, 197; *See also* spiritual eye

F

faculties. *See* capacities

failure, recognizing, 86; transcending, 67-68, 71, 121, 122; in trials, 79; *See also* success

faith, cultivating, 121-122, 138; replaced by knowledge and insight, 149

fantasy, confused with spiritual reality, 58, 61, 124, 169, 170; hallucinations, 57-58; impeding spiritual progress, 78, 98, 155; *See also* daydreaming; illusion

fate, acknowledging of others, 99; affecting spiritual development, 93, 195; factors affecting, 148, 195, 203; of nation and race, 190; of outer world, 67; personal responsibility for, 187; *See also* karma

fear, experienced in dreams, 152; incorrect practice producing, 116, 123; projected feelings producing, 144, 187, 189, 190; reducing, 30, 88, 89, 122, 130, 149; stimulated by awareness, 66

fearlessness, developing, 65-67; *See also* courage

feelings, affecting forms, 141, 142; astral form for, 158, 159; awakening, 49; controlling, 40-42, 44, 47, 53-68, 83, 90, 98, 122; during initiation preparation, 39; during spiritual reflection, 27-28; expressed by objects and animals, 49-50; guidance provided by, 55, 129; in meditation, 34; memory affecting, 125; mental images producing, 62-63; mortal nature of, 200; projection of, 143-144; relationship of to actions, 43, 100, 200; relationship of to outer world, 22-23; relationship of to soul, 21, 176-177; relationship of to thoughts and willing, 57, 59, 176-178, 180,181, 184, 185, 208, 209; severed from ideas, 178; spiritual power of, 43-44, 77; viewing dispassionately, 28, 96; *See also* specific feelings; thoughts

figures, of astral plane, 42, 50-51, 73; revealing inner life, 142-143; revealing spiritual changes, 75

flame-form, of spiritual perceptions, 64

flower, astral form of, 42; *See also* plants

folk soul, 191, *See also* soul

forbearance. *See* tolerance

forces, constructive vs. destructive, 66-67, 115; of courage and fearlessness, 66; for deciphering occult script, 72-73; of desire, 87; development of, 54, 57, 111, 136; directing

spiritual colors, 22
spiritual eye, developing, 50, 51,
    54; opening, 20, 29, 71, 87,
    88, 91, 197; revelations of, 29,
    75; *See also* eye; seeing
spiritual form, 40-43, *See also*
    forms
spiritual literature. *See* occult
    writings
spiritual perception. *See* percep-
    tions
spiritual progress. *See* progress
spiritual researchers. *See* teach-
    ers
spiritual scales, 101
spiritual science, four faculties
    of, 137-138; maintaining faith
    in, 147
spiritual world; confused with
    physical world, 60; establish-
    ing personal place in, 157;as
    prototype for physical world,
    155, 156, 158; *See also* higher
    worlds
steadfastness, cultivating, 101
stimulants, craving for, 129
stone, forces acting upon, 49,
    50; spiritual colors of, 51; *See
    also* crystals; minerals
stranger, self viewed as, 32
strength, contemplation enhanc-
    ing, 29-30, 32, 35; courage en-
    hancing, 66; developing, 17,
    28; devotion enhancing, 18;
    discovering within oneself, 78;
    and endurance, 101, 121, 138;
    initiation enhancing, 72; re-
    quired in training, 103, 187
student. *See* initiate

subsensible world, experiences
    of, 210
subservience, 17
success, differentiating from
    duty, 101; differentiating
    from spiritual progress, 105;
    See also failure
suffering, bearing magnani-
    mously, 71; experienced by
    impure soul, 160; experienc-
    ing dispassionately, 27-28,
    122; expressed in sound, 45;
    individual portion of, 185;
    spiritual dimension of, 35;
    See also experience; feelings
sun rise, affecting feelings, 41
superiority, suppressing feelings
    of, 47
supernatural, individual capaci-
    ties for, 74
supersensible worlds. *See*
    higher worlds
superstition, 78, 88, 207
symbolism, expressed in
    dreams, 151-152; expressed
    in transience, 138; in spiritual
    language, 26, 165, 212, 213
sympathy, reverence awaken-
    ing, 22; *See also* empathy

T
tact, developing, 89-90, 118
talents. *See* capacities
tasks. *See* responsibilities
teachers, 14-15; forces ex-
    pressed by, 48-49, 136; for
    meditation, 35-36; outgrow-
    ing need for, 174; physical

spiritual dimension of, 35, 104, 175; *See also* responsibilities

world. *See* higher worlds; outer world

writings. *See* occult writings

Z
Zanoni, 189n1

DURING THE LAST TWO DECADES of the nineteenth century the Austrian-born Rudolf Steiner (1861–1925) became a respected and well-published scientific, literary, and philosophical scholar, particularly known for his work on Goethe's scientific writings. After the turn of the century he began to develop his earlier philosophical principles into an approach to methodical research of psychological and spiritual phenomena.

His multifaceted genius has led to innovative and holistic approaches in medicine, science, education (Waldorf schools), special education, philosophy, religion, economics, agriculture (Biodynamic method), architecture, drama, new arts of eurythmy and speech, and other fields. In 1924 he founded the General Anthroposophical Society, which today has branches throughout the world.

For prices and a catalogue of titles published and distributed
by the Anthroposophic Press, please write to:

ANTHROPOSOPHIC PRESS,
3390 ROUTE 9, HUDSON, NY 12534
TEL: 518-851-2054
website: www.anthropress.org
e-mail: anthropres@aol.com